Greenhill Books

TWELVE DAYS ON
THE SOMME

Camp 34. Trones Wood

TWELVE DAYS
ON THE SOMME

A Memoir of the Trenches, 1916

SIDNEY ROGERSON

Foreword by Commander Jeremy Rogerson

Introduction by Malcolm Brown

Greenhill Books, London
MBI Publishing, St Paul

Greenhill
Books

This edition first published in 2006 by Greenhill Books/Lionel Leventhal
Ltd, Park House, 1 Russell Gardens, London NW11 9NN
and
MBI Publishing Co., Galtier Plaza, Suite 200, 380 Jackson Street, St Paul,
MN 55101-3885, USA

*CIP data records for this title is are available from the
British Library and the Library of Congress*

ISBN-13 978-1-85367-680-2
ISBN-10 1-85367-680-2

Frontispiece: 'Camp 34, Trones Wood' by Stanley Cursiter

Printed and bound in Great Britain by the MPG Books Group

"Then appeared the iron king crowned with his iron helm, with sleeves of iron mail on his arms. . . . and round him and behind him rode his men armed as nearly like him as they could fashion themselves; so iron filled the fields and the ways and the sun's rays were in every quarter reflected from iron."

Old Parisian Chronicler

CONTENTS

FOREWORD

As THE ELDEST of Sidney Rogerson's three children,
I was asked by Michael Leventhal of Greenhill Books
to give a brief account of my father from a family per-
spective. He was born, the eldest son of a country
parson, in Winterborne Kingston, Dorset, in 1894, and
at the age of six the family moved to Yorkshire where
they were to live for the next fifteen years. This was
perhaps the most influential period of his life, when he
developed a deep love and knowledge of the countryside around him, and for the local inhabitants, which
was to remain with him throughout his life. After
school at Worksop College, Nottinghamshire, he went
up to Sidney Sussex College, Cambridge, on a
Modern History Exhibition in 1912, but on the out-
break of war he left to join the West Yorkshire
Regiment without completing his degree, although he
was subsequently awarded his BA after the war. Time
at university was spent mainly on the cricket and
soccer pitches, and in addition he used his flair for
drawing cartoon sketches to illustrate various college
menus and the like. Indeed, he harboured designs on
joining the Slade and becoming an artist, but all that
changed with his wartime experiences in the trenches.
Two of his sketches drawn at the time are included in
this book.

After the war he went into public relations and

joined the Federation of British Industries, the fore-runner of the present CBI, becoming publicity manager. In 1930 he moved to ICI where he started the publicity department and remained as the manager for over twenty years, before retiring in 1954 to take up a new position in the War Office as Advisor to the Director of Public Relations at the personal request of the prime minister, Winston Churchill. Later he became an honorary colonel in the Territorial Army.

Twelve Days was the first of seven books that he wrote, and it was received with acclaim as the first real account of life in the front line by someone who had actually lived through it, although it took seventeen years before he could bring himself to recount the horrors of life at the time. Writing fiction never appealed to him, but his interest in a broad sweep of other subjects is reflected in his books, which range from *The Old Enchantment*, a series of sketches of country life published in 1938, to *Propaganda in the Next War*, also published in 1938 and which was greeted with considerable interest in Germany. His last book was *Wilfred Rhodes*, a biography of that great Yorkshire and England cricketer, which came out in 1960. After suffering a massive stroke my father spent the last two years in hospital and died in 1968.

What I remember most about him was his sense of fun and his interest in people from all walks of life. At heart he was essentially a countryman, and even in the 1930s he hated to see the indiscriminate growth of suburbia and its effect on the English landscape. He had boundless energy and was game for anything. One endearing example of this occurred when I was serving as Navigation Officer of HMS *St Kitts*, a Battleclass destroyer based in Malta. After taking part in the Suez Operation of 1956 we were due to return to the UK, and my father decided he would like to come with us. My captain granted permission for him to take passage but the only available accommodation was in my two-berth cabin, where for the next ten days he occupied the bottom bunk with me above. Since we were due to return to Plymouth, and my father needed to get back to London as quickly as possible, off Ushant we passed him across at sea by jackstay transfer to our sister ship HMS *Saintes*, which was heading for Portsmouth. Not bad going for a sixty-two year old!

There was rarely a dull moment when he was around, and to complete the picture I have asked Dr James Hayes to add his thoughts and recollections. James, a retired colonial civil servant and, like my father, an author, first met him in Gibraltar in 1954 when James was serving as a national-service subaltern in a Yorkshire regiment and was detailed off to look after my father during his short visit. Later, James became a close friend to all the family, and despite the age difference he and my father were in many ways kindred spirits with a number of shared interests. His views are given below:

"As I found out on his visit to 'The Rock', Sidney Rogerson was especially good with Yorkshire folk and at drawing people out, and nowhere is this humanity and his multiple talents demonstrated so strongly as in *Twelve Days*. His keen powers of observation, his retentive almost photographic memory, allied to his ability to tell a good story and to paint word-pictures in the most memorable prose, are all evident in this book. The varied subject matter of his other books affirms his wide range of interests, in each of which he was exceedingly well informed and had something useful to say. He showed a great interest in the study of eighteenth-century military officers, and also encouraged me to write about my own brief experience of active service in Korea. This I might never have done without his pointing the way in *Twelve Days*, with its descriptions of normal life in the line and the lengthy moves up and down, which became one of the classic accounts of the Great War.

"When I was back at university in London, Sidney took me under his wing, and he readily assented to be one of my referees for a Colonial Service appointment in Hong Kong. During the two years before I left I spent many happy weekends with the Rogerson family in Suffolk, travelling up and down with Sidney. During this period I got to learn much more about him and the sources of his inspiration and achievements. Sidney Rogerson was a big man in mind and body. Ever forthright, he did not suffer fools gladly, not endearing himself to some people in the process, but to those who appreciated him for what he was and what he stood for, he was a beacon. Looking back over half a century later I feel immensely privileged to have known him at an important stage of my life."

JEREMY ROGERSON
2006

INTRODUCTION

I SUSPECT that most people casually picking up this volume and glancing through its pages will immediately assume that it is yet another predictable diatribe against the horrors of the First World War. Here we go again: mud, lice, rats, squalor, futility, protest—the same old mixture as before. In fact, it *is* a book of protest, but not against the war; rather, against the way the war had come to be interpreted when the surge of novels, memoirs and other writings which have become the iconic classics of that conflict caught the headlines from the late 1920s onwards.

The date of its publication is highly significant. *Twelve Days* was published in 1933 and represents a determined attempt to hold back what by then had become an immensely powerful tide. In the wake of the Armistice of November 1918 there had been a widespread acceptance that, despite the suffering and sacrifice it had entailed, the war had been necessary and had been worthily and honourably won. By the time Rogerson took up his pen, however, it was evident that this attitude had undergone a serious transformation. What had taken place has been well described in a recent incisive study of the subject by an American historian, Professor Janet S. K. Watson:

In 1914–1918, you were recognized in many social venues as a worthy (if not necessarily equal) participant in the war—whether you were a soldier, a VAD [i.e. a lady volunteer nurse], a munitions worker, or a bandage roller. By the twentieth anniversary of the beginning of the conflict, however, the popular definition of culturally legitimate war experience had narrowed to that of the soldier in the trenches: young junior officers or possibly men in the ranks, preferably serving in France or Belgium, and almost certainly disillusioned.[*]

As for the four-year-long wrestling match which had taken place in that crucial area of those two countries known to history as the Western Front, it had by then come to be seen as "a pointless, static conflict over strips of earth, which achieved nothing other than the slaughter of millions of young men from both sides".[†]

The names of the books which had commandeered the agenda scarcely need listing, for to a substantial degree they hold the field to this day. Prominent among them were Edmund Blunden's *Undertones of War*, published in 1928; Erich Maria Remarque's *All Quiet on the Western Front*, Robert Graves's *Goodbye to All That* and Richard Aldington's *Death of a Hero*, all published in 1929; and Henry Williamson's *Patriot's Progress* and Siegfried Sassoon's *Memoirs of an Infantry Officer*, both published in 1930. Adding to the mix was R. C. Sherriff's play *Journey's End*, first staged in 1928, and Wilfred Owen's poems, which began their sus-

[*] Janet S. K. Watson, *Fighting Different Wars: Experience, Memory, and the First World War in Britain*, Cambridge University Press, 2004, p. 185.
[†] Watson, p. 1.

tained emotional impact in an edition by Edmund Blunden of 1931.

This was the context in which Sidney Rogerson, former infantry officer, proud member of the West Yorkshire Regiment (The Prince of Wales's Own), and veteran of the Somme and of the arduous but ultimately successful campaigns of 1917–18, began his fight-back. He puts his cards on the table in his Introduction, forcefully and without equivocation:

> The war, it seems, was many wars. There was the grim-smiling-faces-of-undaunted-boys' war of the early correspondents with attacking battalions dribbling footballs across a sporting No-Man's-Land. There was the Generals' war, of the clean map-squares, in which there was never any muddle, no one was ever afraid, and the troops always advanced, by the right, in perfect formation, "as if on parade." Even when they came back again, as they not infrequently did, they retired reluctantly, in good order, dressed by the left. Recently there has been the war of the Sewers, in which no one ever laughed, those who were not melancholy mad were alcoholically hysterical, and most of the action took place in or near the crude latrines of the period.

This is strong stuff, which he clearly hoped would have some effect. "This post-war propaganda," he argues in a further angry paragraph, "piling corpse on corpse, heaping horror on futility, seems bound to fail from every point of view." In fact, as has already been implied, the cause was being lost even as Rogerson threw his weight behind it; the new disenchantment would oust the old certainties and become the generally accepted doctrine for the foreseeable future.

Though not without strong and eloquent support for his case, as we shall see.

Who was he, this forceful, thoughtful, determined, eloquent young ex-officer, hitherto unknown as a writer, taking on those whom he saw as his enemies, like a latter-day Beowulf out to confront his Grendel?

As has been explained in the Foreword, Sidney Rogerson, a parson's son, was born in 1894, lived much of his youth in Yorkshire, and was educated at Worksop College, Nottinghamshire, and Sidney Sussex College, Cambridge, where he read for a BA in Modern History. A member of the Cambridge University Officers Training Corps, he was commissioned into the West Yorkshire Regiment on 14 August 1914, just eight days after the start of the war against Germany. Unlike many of his kind, however, he was spared an early baptism of fire; indeed, whereas thousands of the volunteers of 1914 found themselves poised for action in front-line trenches on the morning of 1 July 1916—the first day of the Battle of the Somme—he was still in England at that point, yet to see a shot fired in anger. He sailed for France on 20 July, as one of several hundred reinforcements intended for his regiment's second battalion, which had gone into action as twenty-one officers and 702 other ranks on 1 July, to be reduced to five officers and 212 other ranks by the end of the day.

By this time a lieutenant, he was posted to B Company, which he later commanded. Like many other battalions which suffered heavily on 1 July 1916, the 2nd West Yorkshires were withdrawn to recover and retrain, returning to the front in the final phase of a campaign which lasted overall for over four and a half months, from 1 July to 18 November. *Twelve Days* is

Rogerson's narrative of a period of front-line duty in November, the battle being on the edge of closedown when they were instructed to withdraw. There were no over-the-top attacks during this period, no trench raids, no fierce flurries of action. Rather, it was a case of determinedly holding the line whatever the conditions or the casualties. To catch the character of the campaign in this grim final phase there can surely be no better description than that coined by Captain J. C. Dunn in his outstanding war diary of the 2nd Royal Welch Fusiliers (the battalion of Siegfried Sassoon and Robert Graves), long famous as *The War the Infantry Knew*. He called it "The Pitiless Somme", a phrase which says it all.

Yet for Rogerson this was no cause for anger. Hence his comment on what he described as "one of the remarkable characteristics of the British soldier— when by every law of nature he should have been utterly weary and 'fed-up' he invariably managed to be almost truculently cheerful" (p. 130). Hence too his ability to find satisfaction in pleasures that seemed even better for the circumstances in which they were enjoyed, as in this passage, brimming, almost literally, with nostalgia: "How the keen edge of appreciation of creature comforts is blunted by a life of peace! Did not a mess-tin of stew, a tot of rum or whisky and water in a tin mug, taste more like divine nectar than the best champagne drunk out of the finest cut-glass to-day?" (p. 96). Summing up his attitude in a keynote passage in his Introduction, which might challenge the assumptions of many people today, he stated: "Life in the trenches was not all ghastliness. It was a compound of many things; fright and boredom, humour, comradeship, tragedy, weariness, courage, and despair."

He even found occasion to chronicle the battalion's experience with pencil and paper, in a style more than a little reminiscent of that of the master of First World War caricature, Bruce Bairnsfather, who was himself a front-line infantry officer as well as an artist. It gives the publishers and myself great pleasure to be able to include here two sketches by Sidney Rogerson, drawn during the twelve days of the book's title, one dated 7 November and the other 15 November, reproduced with the permission and encouragement of the Rogerson family. If nothing else these drawings, never before published, show that their author could find laughter, even comedy, in a situation which we would now tend to assume to have been almost unendurably horrific.

However, let us be clear about one central aspect of Sidney Rogerson's sincerely held creed. He was far from being an uncritical supporter of the way the war on the Western Front had been fought. He was, for example, forthright in his criticism of the practice of senior generals to make their dispositions without adequate knowledge of the actualities of the fighting fronts:

> One of the war's greatest tragedies was that the High Command so seldom saw for themselves the state of the battle zone. What could the men at G.H.Q. who ordered the terrible attacks on the Somme know of the mud from their maps? If they had known, they could never have brought themselves to believe that human flesh and blood could so nearly achieve the impossible, and often succeed in carrying out orders which should never have been issued. [pp. 29–30]

"The Non-Stop to Berlin"
bids. H. Bottomley.

PERKINS LEATHER

2-DAYS RATIONS

CAUCHON

OIL

BOMBS STOKES

GRENA HAND No.5 MARK

L.GUN.
S.A.A. M.E.VII

(CITADEL CAMP)
Nov: 7th

"Each Battn. will on going into the Trenches carry in as many trench-Boards as possible"

"In view of the increasing danger from Trench-feet, a bottle of whale-oil should when possible be supplied to each man"

"Stokes guns play an important part in the attack and each relief must bring with it a proportionate number of Stokes ammunition"

"Two days rations will be carried by every man"

"Whenever possible spare S.A.A will be carried for the use of Lewis guns"

and

"Rifle-fire is becoming more & more important!"

Nor does Rogerson pull his punches in regard to that regular butt of soldierly anger, the army staff. His criticism was not, however, a conventional moan against the staff's perceived incompetence or insensitivity; it was a specific criticism of a specific policy at a particular time, i.e. the three months following the shattering experience on the Somme's first day, which was also the period when he himself finally evolved from untried trainee in the reserve to active soldier in the field. Instead of being given the chance to regroup and recover in decent trenches, the battalion was moved to what he called "the putrid boneyard of Vermelles", part of that grim industrial area to the north of the Somme where the previous year's Battle of Loos had been fought and lost:

> This is the charge that must be laid at the door of the higher staff, that it kept troops with no strategic or tactical advantage in that giant memorial to its own failure, the Loos battlefield, instead of withdrawing them to clean ground where some adequate trench system could be constructed which would enable them to observe and hold the enemy and at the same time to cut down the high daily toll of lives. [pp. 5–6]

One other viewpoint clearly held by Rogerson and his comrades which might challenge received opinions is that there is no sign of that bloodlust, that virulent attitude to the foe, which has become the stuff of fierce academic argument in recent years. He writes, "The English soldier could not hate his enemies for long," citing an occasion when, unable to move for two days in water-logged trenches, the men insisted on sharing their infrequent mugs of tea with a wounded

German. " '. . . Here's a drop of tea for Fritz,' the men would say, as they propped up the captive and fed him as a nurse would feed a patient" (pp. 60–1).

This reminiscence prompted Rogerson to one of his most memorable affirmations (remarkable in a man who was himself brought up with a strong Christian background and who after the war was to take up a career in the field of public relations):

> We were privileged, in short, to see a reign of goodwill
> among men, which the piping times of peace, with all
> their organised charity, their free meals, free hospitals,
> and Sunday sermons have never equalled. Despite all
> the propaganda for Christian fellowship and inter-
> national peace, there is more animosity, uncharitable-
> ness, and lack of fellowship in one business office now
> than in a brigade of infantry in France then. Otherwise,
> we could never have stood the strain. [p. 61]

How was the book received on publication, which took place in November 1933, just in time for the annual Armistice commemorations? It attracted enor-mous attention. Rogerson's own meticulously com-piled scrapbook, now held with numerous other papers in the Documents Department of the Imperial War Museum, teems with evidence of a range of response about which most writers today could only dream. The *Daily Express* serialised it, the first instal-ment being printed on Armistice Day itself. The Prince of Wales, the future Edward VIII, was quoted as having accepted the book as "a welcome addition to [my] library". The former war leader, David Lloyd George, wrote personally to Rogerson, telling him: "Your remarkably vivid book . . . gives a better understanding of the point of view of the fighting soldier than almost anything I have read." The reviewer in the *Sphere* commented: "I hope every Englishman will read it and [that] he will hand it on to some English boy." In similar terms, the reviewer in the *Sunday Times* expressed the hope that "perhaps the book will at least help the younger to understand the older men. Certainly it is worth their while to read it because a more genuine and unbiased account of trench warfare would be hard to find."

Significantly, the book's place in the then current literary spectrum, especially its relation to the surge of disenchanted war literature, did not go unnoticed. Borrowing Rogerson's own striking phraseology as quoted earlier, the *News Chronicle* stated: "The war novelists [*sic*] are divided into two classes—those who think the soldiers in the line were besotted brutes and those who treat them in a brighter vein as adventurous heroes. Mr Sidney Rogerson's *Twelve Days* is a protest against the sewer school in which no one ever laughed ...' etc., etc. In the opinion of the *Birmingham Post*, the book "belongs to an earlier period of war writings, before the demand for the squalid had set in after *All Quiet*", the reviewer, be it noted, not feeling the need to give the full title of Remarque's ground-breaking work because of its obvious celebrity. Similarly, a magazine called *Everyman* gave the book reasonable but far from effusive praise, the reviewer describing himself as "preferring Blunden's equally truthful pages". The *Glasgow Herald*'s reviewer struck a slightly different note, musing that the book seemed "a little blind to the point of view of those more highly strung creatures who were oppressed to the edge of madness by the beastliness of the whole business".

All this might seem to the present-day reader a storm in a distant literary teacup were it not for one important aspect of the war-book war that has not yet been discussed. Here the necessary voice to listen to is that of one of the most forceful and challenging of military and political historians writing today, Correlli Barnett, whose "case" against the revisionists of the late 1920s and early 1930s was first made in his cogent work *The Collapse of British Power*, published in 1972. It is necessary to know that he propounds his argument with due caution, stating: "This is a delicate topic for a historian who has never known a battlefield, for he is sitting in judgement on men who endured ordeals that he fears he himself could not support. The author approaches these writers in personal humility, and in wonder at their courage and fortitude."

Having made clear his position, however, he goes on to argue in commanding terms that the determination of such writers to tell what they saw as the real truth about the war could have dangerous consequences which they could not have foreseen:

> Thus whereas the trench reminiscences began to appear in an epoch when they seemed the belated truth about an experience which now belonged completely to the past, they continued to appear in a new epoch where they had an immediate relevance to the present and the future. What began as an epitaph ended as a warning. As a warning, the war books seemed to say that war was so terrible and futile that the British ought to keep out of another one at any cost.*

* Correlli Barnett, *The Collapse of British Power*, Eyre Methuen, London, 1972, p. 435.

How does Rogerson stand in relation to this pattern of argument? Here it is important to stress once more when the book was published. We can see with hindsight that by 1933 the threat of another war was beginning to raise its head, since that year saw the rise to power of the Nazi party in Germany, under a leader, Adolf Hitler, who was himself fashioned by and, indeed, intellectually distorted by, his own experiences of the Western Front war.

The answer is that Rogerson had himself foreseen what might be described as the pacifist dilemma and had made it an important theme in his book. It becomes a matter of serious discussion in the final chapter, in which he quotes the opinion of a fellow officer killed later in the war, Peter Palmes: "It's better to face up to it, and be ready to defend your life and your heritage rather than lie down and bleat about peace while some one walks roughshod over you" (p. 163).

Building on that statement Rogerson continues in a trenchant passage:

At the time we only felt that Palmes was expressing very succinctly sentiments with which we all agreed, even if we had not thought of them in quite the same dispassionate way, but I have tried to record his remarks as fully as possible since they seem to have a special significance in these after-days. Gathering resonance with the years, they echo out of the mist and mud of that Somme upland with all the force of prophetic warning. What would Peter Palmes, farmer by nature, and warrior by necessity, have had to say could he have lived into the post-war era and seen how Youth attempts to ensure peace by refusing to look on reality. Are we not as a nation behaving very much like the small boy who, alarmed at noises in the dark, will cover his head with his bedclothes lest he see that of which he is terrified? [p. 163]

It is a powerful case, yet the sad fact is that view-points such as Rogerson's had their brief hour of fame and were then overwhelmed by the prevailing tide. The impact of *Twelve Days* seems to have been a transitory one. In 1937 Rogerson published an equally fine book on the Aisne campaign in 1918, when his 8th Division, sent to what was thought to be a quiet sector after surviving two of Germany's make-or-break offensives in March and April, found itself in the path of another massive onslaught in May. Entitled *The Last of the Ebb*, this book was bold enough to include in it, by special invitation, an account of the campaign by a German general; indeed, it even numbered among its dedicatees "our friends the enemy", thus attempting to strike a note of reconciliation between Britons and Germans decades before such gestures would again become possible. Yet that work too has been largely forgotten. His name does not readily occur in books reflecting on the literature of the inter-war years. There is, for example, no place for him in Samuel Hynes's magisterial survey of the First World War and English culture, *A War Imagined*. Nor does the redoubtable Paul Fussell find space for him in his much lauded, highly influential volume *The Great War and Modern Memory*. This only emphasises, however, that he is long overdue for a return to the public stage. In this context Greenhill's decision to reprint this book in time for the ninetieth anniversary of the Battle of the Somme is a worthy and honourable one.

I hope readers will forgive me if I end this Introduction on a personal note. When Greenhill

Books invited me to write it I accepted at once. This was because I have known and admired this book for over thirty years. My first foray into the matter of the Battle of the Somme was a television documentary which I wrote and directed for the BBC to coincide with the battle's sixtieth anniversary in 1976. I was aware as I was devising it that, being scheduled for late June that year, it would inevitably concentrate almost exclusively on the battle's opening phase, in particular on the disastrous attack of 1 July 1916. Yet I did not feel able to do anything like justice to the battle unless I had also studied its frequently overlooked later stages. The Somme was not, after all, a one-day encounter, but a prolonged campaign running from high summer almost to the edge of winter, none of its phases being significantly less important than any other.

During the period of research and production I had two principal allies, to whom I have been conscious ever since of a very great debt. One of these was Martin Middlebrook, whose pioneering work *The First Day on the Somme*, first published in 1971, has long been recognised as a modern First World War classic; additionally it was Martin who first introduced me to the terrain of the Somme and was my consultant throughout the making of the programme.

The second was that remarkable character, the diligent, ever enthusiastic Rose E. B. Coombs, then Special Collections Officer at the Imperial War Museum, and heavily engaged at that time in the last stages of preparing for publication her outstanding guide to the Western Front, *Before Endeavours Fade*, which first appeared in print in August 1976 and has long been an indispensable vade mecum for serious visitors to the French and Belgian battlefields. In one of my numerous conversations with her about the Somme I asked her if she could name one book above any other which would allow me to come to grips with the campaign's final phase. Without hesitation she answered, "*Twelve Days.*" I accepted her advice, read the book, and, it could almost be said, never looked back. This Introduction, therefore, is not only a tribute to Sidney Rogerson; it also offers me a welcome opportunity to pay tribute to the memory of the late, unforgettable Rose Coombs.

All that remains is briefly to celebrate Sidney Rogerson's further career. As already indicated, he was much involved in publicity and public relations, working at various times for the Federation of British Industries, ICI and the Army Council at the War Office. He travelled widely in Europe, Canada and the United States. He contributed to a rich variety of papers and periodicals and was the author of a number of highly esteemed works other than those on military subjects, including such titles as *The Old Enchantment*, *Propaganda in the Next War*, *Our Bird Book* and *Both Sides of the Road*. One of his greatest interests was cricket, especially Yorkshire cricket, his last publication being a biography of that great Yorkshire-born England all-rounder Wilfred Rhodes. To write its Introduction he secured the services of none other than than the great Australian batsman Sir Donald Bradman. Being myself a Yorkshire-born cricket aficionado, if a player of minimal talent, it gives me a special pleasure to be able to claim that I share with the great Sir Don the privilege of having contributed an Introduction to one of Sidney Rogerson's books.

MALCOLM BROWN
2006

AUTHOR'S INTRODUCTION

JESTING PILATE, with a surer eye for the enduring, might have inquired, "What is War?" There have been almost as many answers as there were individuals who knew the Great War directly, not to mention the second-hand versions, plain and coloured, of those who passed on such tales as we chose to tell. The war, it seems, was many wars. There was the grim-smiling-faces-of-undaunted-boys' war of the early correspondents with attacking battalions dribbling footballs across a sporting No-Man's-Land. There was the Generals' war, of the clean map-squares, in which there was never any muddle, no one was ever afraid, and the troops always advanced, by the right, in perfect formation, "as if on parade." Even when they came back again, as they not infrequently did, they retired reluctantly, in good order, dressed by the left. Recently there has been the war of the Sewers, in which no one ever laughed, those who were not melancholy mad were alcoholically hysterical, and most of the action took place in or near the crude latrines of the period.

The simple soldier smiled as he read about himself in the heroics of the war scribes. The bemused survivor is slightly irritated to find his experiences exploited by marrow-freezing agents of peace for all time. Propaganda, during the war, if it failed to reach the fighting man, found its mark at home; England had no lack of civilian warriors who became increasingly bloodthirsty in proportion as the fighting man's appetite for battle grew feebler with every leave. But this post-war propaganda, piling corpse on corpse, heaping horror on futility, seems bound to fail from every point of view. In its distortion, the soldier looks in vain for the scenes he knew. On the other hand, Youth, the target presumably of these peace missiles, remains unpunctured. Youth is not to be beaten into brotherliness by bladders of scarifying sound. Bogies tend always to degenerate into buffoons. The "Corsican ogre" of one year is the tubby "Boney" of the next. The figure which awed the statesmen of one generation is the nursery pantaloon of their grandchildren. Time effaces the mental scars as rapidly as the grass covers the shell-holes. Tin soldiers and toy howitzers are as popular to-day as ever they were, though it is true that no enterprising manufacturer has yet turned out a working model of a gas projector. Meanwhile the world in strict self-defence arms itself against itself, just as before, and the balance of power is again turning in the scale of might.

Secondly, propaganda must be based on truth if it is to succeed over a long period, and to represent the war as one long nightmare is to exaggerate one aspect at the expense of the other.

The description in the following pages is entirely without propagandist urge or intention. It is a plain, unvarnished account of one short tour in the Somme trenches during the winter of 1916, written in the hope of recalling to the soldier the scenes with which he was familiar, and of presenting the younger generations with an accurate picture of life as we lived it in those days. And life in the trenches was not all ghastliness. It was a compound of many things; fright and boredom, humour, comradeship, tragedy, weariness, courage, and despair. Those who were lucky lived, and every six or nine months saw most of their friends die. Soon, the places were filled and the daily round went on. Any description of a long period must focus attention on the high lights, the whirl of battle, the shock of raid and mine. It must skip the lengthy, humdrum and frequently amusing intervals. A short tour, such as that dealt with here, while not less terrible or more amusing than another, condenses into swifter drama the common experience, and leaves room for some background of detail. In the record here set down nothing has been consciously added or exaggerated and nothing material has been left out. Not to weary the reader, one eventless day on the way into the line and one coming out have been omitted, but otherwise every person and incident is real, and everything, including the conversations, is set down in its context.

SIDNEY ROGERSON
1933

I

UP THE LINE

I

UP THE LINE

It was a cold night. There had been snow during the day, and at dusk the wind had risen. Just to complicate matters the camp warden had caught the servants looting the old German dug-outs for firewood, so we had been forced to fill our brazier with ration coal. The result was that the bell-tent which served as B Company's officers' mess and sleeping quarters was filled with a maximum of smoke for a minimum of warmth, and the three of us, with soot-blackened faces and aching lungs, lay in our flea-bags and smoked, and sipped whisky and water out of tin cups, and cursed and discussed the latest rumours—wonderful rumours that we were to entrain shortly for Italy, for Salonika, for any other front but the Somme.

It was the evening of November 7, 1916, when the Somme offensive was spluttering out in a sea of mud. The place was Citadel Camp, a dreary collection of bell-tents pitched insecurely on the hillside near the one-time village of Fricourt. Our unit was the 2nd Battalion of the West Yorkshire Regiment. Although I was officer commanding B Company, I had actually less experience of France than either of the others, who both wore the 1914 Star. Mac, the senior of the two, was a lean, youthful Irishman, whose character-

3

istics were a cynical sense of humour and an astonishing cool courage which, being observed by those
in authority, caused him to be singled out to lead
raids, to crawl about on his belly in No-Man's-
Land, or to undertake any single-handed exploit of
a perilous nature. He had enlisted as a mere boy,
and had been sent at once to the signal section
attached to one of the Indian Divisions. He had
been posted to us with a commission about three
months previously. George Hall was a very
different type. Whereas Mac and I were in our
very early twenties, he was over thirty—a real
Yorkshireman, stubborn, stolid, and cheerful. After
years of service in the ranks of the regiment he had
been commissioned, and made a very conscientious,
dependable officer.

We were all lucky to be the possessors of a sense
of humour which persisted in rising equally above
the various forms of boredom which beset us and
the many manifestations of " frightfulness " which
the enemy and the staff visited upon us. Still,
though we could laugh heartily at ourselves as a
trio of blackamoors, we were tired, like the majority
of the Battalion—mentally rather than physically,
for our condition was splendid. This was the
regiment's second experience of the " Blutbad."
Some of us remembered that sunny last evening in
June when we had assembled with such high hopes
in the trenches opposite Ovillers La Boiselle. How
we had jested and joked, even collecting pieces of
chalk wherewith to label as our own trophies the
guns we were so sure of taking ! Some of us too,
remembered the next night, when, with every officer
but one a casualty, and our dead hanging thick on

the German wire, we had been withdrawn, sweating and shaking and shattered. It had taken us three months to recover from that blow—three months which had been spent in that putrid boneyard around Vermelles, where the front was a maze of trenches old and new, German, French, and British ; trenches blown in and disused or abandoned and derelict ; British fire trenches which had once been German communication trenches ; trenches ending in saps twenty yards from the enemy line ; salients, re-entrants, and fortified mine craters—all reeking of death and stagnation. Men vomited over the task of digging new trenches, for bodies were unearthed at every yard. The deepening of the front line turned a German officer out of the mud beneath our very feet. A sap led into an overgrown trench full of French skeletons of 1914. Most pitiful, the attempt to straighten a piece of trench broke into a dug-out where sat huddled three Scottish officers, their faces mercifully shrouded by the grey flannel of the gas-masks they had donned when death came upon them. In such places as the Kaiserin trench the parapet was revetted with corpses thinly hidden by rotting sandbags whence at night the rats fled squeaking from their ghoulish repasts.

This is the charge that must be laid at the door of the higher staff, that it kept troops with no strategic or tactical advantage in that giant memorial to its own failure, the Loos battlefield, instead of withdrawing them to clean ground where some adequate trench system could be constructed which would enable them to observe and hold the enemy and at the same time to cut down the high daily toll of lives. For as things were, the British and German lines were in places only a few yards apart, so that hand grenades could easily be lobbed into them ; sometimes they actually ran into one another, separated only by a trench " stop " of sandbags and barbed wire. Yet for all their closeness they were often out of sight of each other, since the continual explosion of mine and counter-mine had reared great mounds of gleaming chalk high into No-Man's-Land. These craters were hotly debated territory : the scene at night of bloody, silent struggles with knife and trench club ; watched over during daylight by anxious sentry posts, perched at the end of shallow saps, who peered at each other through tiny periscopes clipped on to bayonet blades.

To the terror of the mine from beneath was added the hail of missiles from above, ranging from small hand and rifle grenades, each capable of wiping out a sentry post, through a variety of trench-mortar bombs of medium calibre up to the enormous " minenwerfers." Standing over 3 feet 6 inches in height and filled with nearly two hundred pounds of high explosive, they had a more demoralising effect than any other single form of enemy action. There was no sound of distant discharge to give warning of their coming. Ears had to be sharp indeed to hear the warning whistle blown by the German gunners before they fired their mortars. Eyes had to be fixed in the air to watch for the shape which would soar ponderously upward, turn slowly over and over in its downward flight like a tumbler pigeon, and with a woof ! woof ! woof ! burst with a shattering crash, sending long jagged strips of metal whirring savagely for yards and rending into tiny fragments everything around. The very leisureliness of their descent was demoralising. The uncertainty as to where they would pitch was demoralising. The immense clamour of their explosion was demoralising. But most demoralising was the damage they could do. Men do not easily or soon throw off the shock of seeing all that could be found of four of their comrades carried down for burial in one ground sheet.

It was in such an atmosphere of putrefaction, amid the continual nerve-racking strain of " minenwerfers," of raid and counter-raid, mine and countermine, that we had rested through the warm autumn months. Then, as the leaves fell and the weather began to break, the order had come for us to return to the Somme. Anxiously the men had asked, " Are there any ' minnywoffers ' ? " and had been relieved to get the answer, No. But since then we had done one attack, which, at the loss of six officers and two hundred and thirteen other ranks out of the total of four hundred and thirty-seven who had " gone over the top," had taught us the existence of the new terror of the mud.

It is not strange, therefore, that we were badly in need of rest—not " rest " in the official sense, which meant withdrawing a Battalion from the rigours and dangers of the actual trenches to a camp within the devastated zone, composed of squalid hutments linked up by crazy duckboards and sour from dirt and overcrowding. What we needed was to be sent right out of the battle area, to some quiet village where a man could expel the shell-fumes from his lungs and fill them with the sweet air of the countryside ; where he could rest his tired eyes with the sight of something green after the drab monotony of a battlefield where the constant churning of shells, wheels, and feet had robbed even freshly turned earth of its distinctive colour.

Which was why the three of us were so eagerly discussing the rumours of a move to Italy, and conjured up warm visions of some " cushy " line of trench with the blue Alpine skies above and the limpid Piave below, where " minenwerfers," mustard gas, mines, and mud were unknown, and where warfare was, in fact, still something of the gentleman's business we somehow imagined it ought to be.

A rap on the tent canvas and the announcement of " Battalion Orders, sir," brought us back to reality with a bump. " The Battalion will relieve the 2nd Devon Regiment in the front line on the night of the 10th–11th November. . . ." Each of us received the news in his own way—Mac with an air of " I told you so," George Hall with an adequate Yorkshire curse, and I, as I thought befitting a company commander, with a great show of enforced cheerfulness. Inwardly each of us was equally depressed, and I personally shrank from my task of having to communicate the news to the company, or at least to those who did not already know it !

The sector we were to take over from the Devon Regiment was at the very apex of the salient formed by the offensive, a little to the left of Lesbœufs Wood, and almost exactly opposite what was left of the village of Le Transloy. As the crow flies, Citadel Camp was little more than six miles behind this line, yet such were the conditions that this comparatively short distance had to be accomplished in two stages. To-morrow, orders explained, the Battalion would quit the Citadel and move to other quarters designated merely by a map reference but actually in the particularly unsalubrious locality between Bernafay and Trones Woods. Having passed the gist of these instructions on to Company Sergeant-Major Scott, I turned in to get as much sleep as possible.

Next morning, in torrential rain, burdened with trench impedimenta under waterproof capes, the Battalion trudged wearily out of camp in Indian file, along roads ankle-deep in slush and congested with traffic of all kinds, from strings of sodden pack-mules, ammunition limbers, and " cookers " to ambulances and staff cars. If anything were needed to put the seal of absolute cheerlessness on that move it was the single-file formation. No matter how dismal the present, or hopeless the prospect, a very comforting sense of comradeship can be developed by tramping along in fours. There is a sense of close company ; the ability to talk to your neighbour, even to sing with him. There is the inevitable swing and rhythm of the column. But put men into Indian file and all this corporate cheerfulness evaporates. They develop a spiritless shamble with the whole straggling line continually contracting and expanding, alternately treading on one another's heels, then panting to recover lost distance. So it was on this occasion, with the added discomfort that ever and again a passing vehicle would push men off into the treacherous morass at the roadside so that they sank up to

their waists and were only pulled out with great
effort.   Or a block would occur, and all traffic
stopped while men and horses alike stood silent,
wet, and wretched.

The few whose brains were not too numbed for
thought comforted themselves with the reflection
that at any rate another camp awaited them at the
end of the march.   There would be somewhere to
lie down in dryness and take off one's pulling,
sopping boots.   There would be braziers.   There
would perhaps even be a hot meal ready.

Actually there were none of these things.   There
was not even a camp, at least a camp which was
ready to receive us.   This, and much more of a
most violent nature, was reported to the Colonel
by a very desperate Quartermaster, to whom the
comfort of his beloved regiment was his religion.
Some one had blundered, we knew at once, but,
ignorant of what had actually happened, we shrugged
our shoulders and damned the Staff, who, as the
controllers of our movements and our destinies,
were not unnaturally, though often unfairly, blamed
for everything that went wrong.   Had we known
the truth we might have been angry instead of
philosophically resigned, for on this occasion the
Staff were not the real culprits.   They had neither
sent us to the wrong map reference nor forgotten
to provide us with accommodation.   The trouble
arose from the fact that we were timed to take
over this accommodation an hour earlier than its
sitting tenants, a territorial Battalion of the Scottish
Rifles on its way out of action, were due to vacate
it.   Notwithstanding that they were moving back
towards comfort and safety, these Scotsmen stub-

bornly refused to quit one minute before they were scheduled to do so. To all the blandishments and cajoleries of Hinchcliffe, our Quartermaster, they turned a deaf ear, and not even his argument that the incoming unit was commanded by a Cameronian weighed with them in the slightest. Their observation was that in this war the motto was : " Every man for himself and the de'il tak' the hindmost," to which Hinchcliffe, properly nettled, retorted that that was a game at which two could play, and stamped out with the declaration that it would go ill with the conduct of the war and the happiness of the troops if such a spirit were indeed to gain ground.

In reality it was very seldom that so uncompromising an attitude was encountered between unit and unit, and even in this instance there was some excuse for it in that the " Jocks " had dragged themselves out of the line only the day previously after a terrible mauling. The Battalion had been almost wiped out, and the handful of survivors, a little over a hundred in number, were weary and shaken in body and spirit, and too dejectedly apathetic to rouse themselves to any effort until such was demanded of them by orders.

Of these complications we knew nothing. All we realised was that the usual muddle had taken place. There was nothing to be done. Until the powers that were could find a lodgment for us in that congested wilderness we were more utterly homeless than any waif on London streets. Meanwhile the rain descended remorselessly.

This check occurred at the corner of Bernafay Wood amidst whose shattered trunks and battle filth we fell out until the tangle should be straightened out. Wetter they could not be, but the men were in a most cheerful mood, induced probably by a determination to rise above their surroundings. Huddling together for warmth, they fluently cursed this latest example of what they described as a " proper bloody box-up." One wag started to sing, " When you're all dressed up and nowhere to go, Life seems weary, dreary, and slow ! " *con molto expressione*. And in this way the hour passed, and we slopped off through the mud to take possession of the now vacant " Camp 34."

For two reasons it is difficult to convey a satis-factory impression of that camp's surroundings. First, one had lost the habit of looking afield. This was due to the cramping effect of trench life, where a man was a member of a very small community from which, sleeping or waking, he was never sepa-rated, and was confined for days at a stretch within the narrow limits of a trench. " Keep your head down " was a piece of advice which became second nature, with the result that, metaphorically speaking, he slunk about from hole to hole, from one piece of cover to the next, his head down, not daring, or else forgetting, to look about him. His vision changed, he began to lose the wider view, and instead to see falconwise the minutest details around, details which will ever survive in his memory. How many men who fought and lived around Ypres or Arras for months carry any mental picture of the general aspect of the countryside ? But ask them to describe the Kirchner pictures pinned to the walls of their dug-out, the particular brand of bully-beef tin which hung on the wire, and they will find little difficulty.

Secondly, we had grown accustomed to living in a region where almost every natural landmark had been obliterated. Country that had once been the twin sister of the Sussex Downs, with little comfortable villages nestling round their churches in the folds of the hills, had been battered into a vast monotony of drab. Churches, houses, woods, and hedgerows had all disappeared. Our landmarks were provided for us in the shape of military noticeboards in the back areas, or by such débris as wrecked aeroplanes, derelict tanks, dead horses, and even dead men nearer the front line.

Suffice it, therefore, to say that the camp was situated on an open space of what had once been grassland between the mangled remains of Trones and Bernafay Woods. The distance was shrouded by rain and mist, from out of which the boom of gunfire came distant and muffled.

" Camp 34 " itself was a camp in name only—a few forlorn groups of rude tarpaulin-sheet shelters huddled together, as though they shrank from the surrounding desolation. One or two bell-tents there were, it is true, here and there, but even they looked as unhappy as if they knew themselves to be but insecurely at anchor in the rising sea of mud. Though even these few tarpaulin-sheets and bell-tents might have been sufficient shelter for the pitiful remnant of the Scottish regiment, they were entirely inadequate for a Battalion more or less up to strength. Since no shelter had been prepared for us, necessity forced us to take steps to procure it for ourselves. In other words, we were reduced to looting, or in the more picturesque language of the ranks, " scrounging " additional cover. With

the grim determination of the British soldier, be-
draggled men set off with the hearty approval, if
not the verbal permission, of their officers to see
what they could find. I am not ashamed to confess
that, unofficially, I strongly encouraged the more
experienced soldiers—who were therefore less likely
to be caught !—to scour the dripping countryside
for anything likely to improve the company's
accommodation, and even gave them permission
to leave the camp " to visit the canteen, sir."
Needless to say, that canteen was never discovered,
but other valuable things were.

So far as I was concerned, the first incident was
the arrival of the Colonel, imperturbable as always,
though inwardly raging at the lack of organisation
which subjected men going in to battle to such
experiences. Behind him, looking indescribably
sheepish, stood my young servant, Briggs.

" I congratulate you on your servant," the
Colonel said casually. " Why, sir ? " I queried.
" Well, as I walked into the very commodious trench
shelter reserved for Battalion Headquarters, I saw
your man walking out at the other end with the
stove. And you hadn't been in camp five minutes !
A good boy, that. But I'm sorry I could not spare
the stove ! " The Colonel smiled, and moved on.

Every minute saw an addition to " camp stores,"
the greatest triumph being the purloining, by Privates
Purkiss and Kiddell, from under the very noses
of the rightful owners, of a huge balloon tarpaulin
which proved big enough of itself to house more
than half the company ! In less than a couple of
hours I was satisfied that reasonably dry and warm
quarters had been contrived for every man, of B

Company at least. Meanwhile, a hot meal had been issued from the cookers and—the rain stopped. Spirits began to mount again, and as a setting sun was wanly mirrored in the water-logged shell-holes, snatches of song began to rise with the smoke of braziers from the improvised shelters.

Not least remarkable was the transformation of the bell-tent allotted for Company Headquarters. On arrival this had flapped lugubriously on its sagging ropes over a patch of mud, but within the hour it had been pitched afresh, taut and confident in appearance ; a neighbouring R.E. dump had provided enough new trench boards for a complete floor, and a brazier had been lit.

The enlargement of that camp in so short a time is worthy to rank among the minor miracles of war.

The day closed with an issue of rum. The first stage of the relief was over.

II

TAKING-OVER

II

TAKING-OVER

Next morning we were reluctant to leave the frowsy warmth of our flea-bags, and for once it was left to Mac, usually the last to stir, to crawl out, open the tent-flap, and let in the November mist and cold. As he did so a working-party of dismounted Indian cavalry plodded past, their faces peering, livid and drawn, out of their woollen cap-comforters. Mac had acquired a smattering of " soldier " Hindustani, and called out a greeting, the effect of which was instantaneous, the grey faces lighting up with smiles at the sound of their own tongue spoken, no matter with how vile an accent, in this terrifying, alien wilderness.

The first news that greeted us on arising was that the enemy had been up to some of his " frightfulness " during the night. German planes had not only carried out a raid behind our lines, but a long-range shell had actually hit one of the Battalion cookers and " napooed " it completely. The fact that we had heard neither of these demonstrations is a proof that we had slept soundly ! But we did not like the news about that shell. It must have been uncomfortably near the camp.

After a mournful beginning, the day tried bravely to make amends for its predecessor by being bright and sunny, and the ingenuity of company commanders was tested in devising small parades or exercises which, without worrying the men, should keep them occupied and warm. How often organised activity of this sort is misinterpreted ! For officers as well as men the path of least resistance would have been to do nothing, yet here were close on five hundred men dumped down for the space of forty-eight hours on the equivalent of a ploughed field, soggy with winter rain ; housed in rude shelters into which they had to crawl and in which they could scarcely sit upright ; their only warmth two ration blankets and the body of the next man, and with the dismal prospect of four days of even worse discomfort and considerably more danger to exercise their minds. Left to themselves, what was there for them to do but stand listlessly about or lie, getting hourly more cramped and stiff, in their blankets on the soaked earth ? Better by far that they should be made to busy their brains and their bodies, to wash and shave themselves, to clean their equipment, and to move about on some trivial task or other while the sun shone or daylight lasted.

Moreover, while we had been in Citadel Camp we had received drafts of over two hundred men to replace our losses, and it was therefore essential that these new arrivals should be fitted into their sections and platoons and given a chance to know, by sight at least, the N.C.O.'s and officers under whom they had to go into action. Many of them were Northumbrian miners, " Geordies," whose outlandish Tyneside accents were barely intelligible to our own Yorkshiremen, which made some kind of " getting together " still more necessary.

No one abhorred these forced activities more than

Mac. To George Hall, drill of all kinds was almost second nature, but to Mac it was an utterly incomprehensible waste of time. While George cheerfully bellowed out commands and put his platoon energetically through arms drill or parade movements himself, Mac stood disconsolately, his cap well on the back of his head, his hand for ever stealing to his breeches pocket, watching the N.C.O.'s doing the actual work. Yet bored as he looked as he listened to Company Sergeant-Major Scott's gruff voice monotonously reiterating the bayonet drill, " Point ! Parry ! Short Point ! Parry right !" he had to smile when Scott waxed righteously indignant—" Long point ! Corporal Needham, put more thrust in it ! Point ! "—then, disgustedly, " Corporal Needham, you couldn't stick a sausage ! "

But let us leave them at it—arms drill, bayonet fighting, platoon drill, bomb-cleaning, kit inspections. Useless work, perhaps. Who knows ? Follow me instead to Battalion Headquarters, but walk delicately. Pick your way between the tarpaulin shelters guyed to their screw pickets, and mind the strands of old Boche wire which loop redly out of the mud.

A few weeks ago Battalion Headquarters was a length of German trench. To-day, by the simple expedient of roofing it over with corrugated iron and stopping one end with sandbags, it is a desirable habitation, furnished, it is true, only with a table— of sorts—and two or three wooden frames covered with rabbit-wire, which do duty as beds or chairs as necessity demands. Yet ramshackle as the place sounds, as a winter residence, to us dwellers in the tented field, it is as near luxury as our numbed imaginations can conceive. At the far end, huddled close to the stove coveted by my servant, sits the Colonel, wrapped in the camel's-hair lining of his trench coat, and if I mention him at some length here it is because the prevailing atmosphere of ordered comfort is largely a reflection of his personality.

Colonel Jack was an " importation." He had come to us from the Cameronians, but so completely had he identified himself with us and incidentally endeared himself to us that his alien origin had been completely and quickly forgotten. " A regular soldier of the best type " is the phrase which comes nearest to describing him, but it is inadequate. As punctilious on the parade-ground as he was regardless of his safety and unsparing of his energy in action, he had other and rarer qualities. Something of a martinet, and apt to be querulous on occasions, he was at the same time a real friend to his officers and, through them, to his men. In all ways he set us an example, but if asked to name his peculiar characteristic, I should say it was his determination, from which I never saw him relax, to keep up at all times and at all costs the proprieties of the old life of peace. " There's no need to live like a pig even though one is surrounded by filth, you know," he would say, and he never did. No matter what the circumstances, he was always spick and span, and it was typical of him that before any big attack he would be careful to see that his boots and buttons were polished, explaining with a slow smile that one could " always die like a gentleman—clean and properly dressed."

Excuse the digression, and behold us all gathered to discuss details of the morrow's relief. MacLaren is there, the second-in-command, an officer on the reserve wrenched by the war from the comfortable home in Ontario which he will never see again. A Company is represented by Palmes, a militia captain, who has left a Rhodesian farm and is destined to die on the same day as MacLaren, nine months ahead ; and by his senior subaltern, Arthur Skett, just joined from Sandhurst. I answer for B Company. Hawley, a senior captain of the regiment, plunged into this grim winter campaign after years of service in the steam-heat of West Africa, has C ; and Sankey, a 2nd Lieutenant just promoted from the ranks of the Canadians, is temporarily in command of D Company. Matheson, another promoted Canadian, is acting adjutant.

Preliminaries over, it is disclosed that the Colonel has decided to leave out of the trenches MacLaren and Palmes, whose company will be taken in by Skett. Two company sergeant-majors, including Scott, will also be left at transport lines. The Battalion will take over from the Devons company for company, A and B manning the front or outpost line with C and D in close support. The sector we are to take over lies between what remains of the villages of Lesbœufs and Le Transloy, at the very peak of the Somme salient. The positions occupied by the Devons are, the Colonel admits, " sketchy," and the ground, which has only been won after stubborn local fighting, has been so pounded that, except for short lengths of German line, anything in the nature of a trench is non-existent. It is only possible, in fact, to reach the front line under cover of darkness or the early morning mist.

" Company commanders," the Colonel goes on, " will leave with me before dawn to-morrow so as to get an idea of the line before daylight.   We'll start at 5.30 a.m.   You fellows had better breakfast with me here at 5 a.m. sharp."

Details as to quartermasters' arrangements, hours of relief, rendezvous for guides, etc., are to be given in Battalion Orders, so after we have returned a negative to the Colonel's " Any questions ? " we retire to our respective commands to re-enact the scene on a smaller scale.   Little fleas, indeed.

To Mac fell the responsibility of leading B Company up to the trenches and, in spite of the desperately early start it entailed, I secretly welcomed the Colonel's decision.   " He travels the fastest who travels alone," and speed was safety, especially in crossing that valley to the left of Lesbœufs Wood marked on the maps " Heavily shelled area " !

There being nothing better to do, I was in bed and asleep ridiculously early, though I found it no easier to rise with alacrity when called next morning at 4.30 a.m.   Still half asleep, I struggled into the clothes I was to wear for three days.   I put on trench boots, donned a heavy cardigan, decorated with woolly mascots, under my khaki jacket, and a leather jerkin above it. Over all I buckled on the various items of my " Christmas tree "—gas respirator, water bottle, revolver, and haversack—took a rolled-up ground-sheet instead of an overcoat, wound a knitted scarf round my neck and exchanged my cap for a " battle bowler." With a " Chin-chin, see you later," to Mac and George, I set off with my runner for Battalion Headquarters.

A welcome aroma of coffee greeted me as I entered the dug-out where, in the warm light of the candles, I found the Colonel, Hawley, and Sankey already sitting down to breakfast. Skett arrived shortly after me and apologised for being late. He told me privately that he did not feel well. Certainly he did not look well, and seemed anxious and ill-at-ease. While the rest of us fell to heartily on Sergeant Brownlow's scrambled eggs and bacon and coffee, realising it would be our last decent meal for days, Skett ate practically nothing. We did not, I am afraid, view these symptoms very seriously at the time. It was no new thing for a youngster to be nervous when called on for the first time to take charge of a company in the front line. " Leave him alone and he'll be all right," was Hawley's comment, which we accepted.

Punctually to the hour we set out into the darkness, winding our way along crazy duck-board tracks, past holes in the ground where guttering candles and muffled voices told of human occupation, past dimly-seen gun positions and subterranean dressing-stations until, just as dawn was breaking, we reached the headquarters of the Devon Regiment in the sunken road to the left of Lesbœufs Wood.

It needed the war to demonstrate the full truth of the saying that " joy cometh in the morning." With the passing of darkness a load of danger seemed to be lifted, and even the poor shattered countryside appeared fresh and peaceful in the early morning glow. We were sharply reminded that this was but an illusion, for as we stayed chatting cheerfully, Colonel Sunderland of the Devons came out and told us to get away quickly as the place was a death-trap, " taped " to an inch by enemy gunners.

Each of us got a Devon guide and set off with all haste to reach the comparative safety of our respective destinations before the mist lifted and the early aeroplanes flew over as heralds of the day's shelling. The front line, our guide told us, lay over the low ridge which formed the skyline half a mile ahead, and had only been dug last night. " It's not easy to find in the darkness," he went on in his soft West-country dialect. " In daylight it's all right. You follow this track till you come to a dead Boche. Here he be, zur ! " pointing to a sprawling field-grey body wearing the uniform, I noticed, of the Minenwerfer Corps. " Then you have to look for a white tape—here, zur—and he leads you roight up to behind the old front line. But it's easy to go wrong at noight."

We crossed a low valley where the shell-ploughed ground was carpeted with dead, the khaki outnumbering the field-grey by three to one. There must have been two or three hundred bodies lying in an area of a few hundred yards around Dewdrop Trench—once a substantial German reserve line, but now a shambles of corpses, smashed dug-outs, twisted iron and wire. This was the position which C and D Companies were to take over, and whither Hawley and Sankey made their way with some misgivings.

Skett and I walked on together until we reached the slope, when he veered off to the left and I to the right. The sun was now up and the protective mist had cleared, so that I was glad when I slithered into the shallow trench half-way up the ridge where B Company of the Devons had established their headquarters by the simple expedient of roofing in the trench with two stretchers—which might have kept off a little gentle rain but nothing more substantial ! Tea was being made for breakfast, and though I accepted an offer of refreshment which was very welcome, I turned away retching after the first gulp. It tasted vilely of petrol. For miles in the rear there was no water either fit or safe to drink, and all supplies had therefore to be carried up to the front in petrol tins, a system which was all right only so long as the tins had been burnt out to remove the fumes of the spirit. When they had not, as all too often happened, every mouthful of food and drink was nausea. It was only with the greatest difficulty that men could be restrained from using water from the shell-holes to make their tea or bully-stew, although this was expressly forbidden, as in addition to the danger of gas-poisoning, none knew what horror lay hidden under the turbid water. Having already breakfasted, albeit four hours earlier, I watched Hill, my opposite number of the Devons, eat his bread and " Maconochie," after which, over a cigarette, he explained the situation to me.

The two companies were both posted on the ridge which had been but newly captured, and though their fronts were touching, their flanks were both entirely in the air. The only approximation

to a trench was the one in which we were sitting,
already christened Autumn Trench, which was
merely a narrow, unrevetted channel, without
shelter, or fire-steps, and in which A Company
also had its headquarters some 150 yards to the
left. From this line a shallow trench, nowhere
more than three feet deep, had been scooped out
over the ridge, joining on the far side the real
front line, which had only been established the
night before by linking up shell-hole to shell-hole.
This sketchy line had been made to gain a sight into
the valley at the other side of the ridge, and had
naturally been dug under cover of darkness, but
daylight showed, so I was told, that the ground
fell away so steeply in front of it that complete
observation was still impossible.

That was all Hill had to tell me about our own
defence system, but admitted that the enemy was
in little better straits. In fact, the Hun was not
known to be holding any fixed line nearer than the
Transloy-Bapaume road, some thousand yards
away, though the area between that line and ours
crawled with Germans who hung on in isolated
bits of trench or in fortified shell-holes, the whereabouts of which were extremely difficult to detect.

In short, the position was as obscure as it was
precarious. The two companies were virtually
isolated on their ridge without knowledge of the
exact dispositions of the enemy in front, and
behind them, no trench, just mile after mile of
battered country under its pall of mud. " It's not
a cheerful sort of place to hold," my informant
went on. " All the Boche has got to do is to pop
a barrage down in the valley behind you and come

over on both flanks, and you're marching off to Hunland before you know where you are ! " (A comforting thought, I reflected, but no less than the truth. Isolated as we were, the enemy could bag the lot of us almost before our own Battalion Headquarters half a mile in rear were any the wiser.)

" And now I think I've given you all the facts," he ended, " except that you'll find the mud a bit trying in places. If I were you, I'd have a look round for myself while the Boche is behaving himself."

The front certainly was quiet, save for the occasional sharp whip-crack of an enemy sniper and the drone of aircraft high up in a sky which was very bright and blue for November. It had been strangely peaceful sitting, smoking, and chatting in the sun, but I had not gone twenty yards before I encountered the mud, mud which was unique even for the Somme. It was like walking through caramel. At every step the foot stuck fast, and was only wrenched out by a determined effort, bringing away with it several pounds of earth till legs ached in every muscle.

No one could struggle through that mud for more than a few yards without rest. Terrible in its clinging consistency, it was the arbiter of destiny, the supreme enemy, paralysing and mocking English and German alike. Distances were measured not in yards but in mud.

One of the war's greatest tragedies was that the High Command so seldom saw for themselves the state of the battle zone. What could the men at G.H.Q. who ordered the terrible attacks on the

Somme know of the mud from their maps ? If
they had known, they could never have brought
themselves to believe that human flesh and blood
could so nearly achieve the impossible, and often
succeed in carrying out orders which should never
have been issued.

I had only to struggle some fifty yards before I
came to the communication trench over the ridge,
along which, crouching double or on all fours, we
went for a further fifty yards before finding ourselves in the front line, christened by us, and there-
after known as Fall Trench. This I found to be
better than I expected, already fairly deep and
reasonably dry. I found that there was a detach-
ment of brigade machine gunners there as a welcome
addition to the trench garrison, and floundered
along towards the left till I met Skett, with whom
I compared notes and discussed a working programme for the night. We eventually agreed that
we must at all costs deepen and consolidate Fall
Trench, and run a couple of saps out from it, so
as to command a full view of the valley in front.
Secondly, to protect our flanks, Skett agreed to
put a subaltern into an isolated post on his left,
and I to make a T-head for a Lewis gun-post
opening out on the right of the so-called communication trench to cover that flank. Leaving Skett, I
returned by the way I had come to find that the
round of a few hundred yards had taken over two
hours of strenuous walking !

The impression left on my mind was that we
were as much at the mercy of the elements as of
the enemy. Of the ordinary amenities of trench
life there were none. The two stretchers at Company

Headquarters formed the only roof in the sector. There was not even a hole into which men could crawl to be under shelter. They slept as they sat, huddled into themselves, in positions reminiscent of prehistoric burial. As cooking was out of the question, there was no apology for a cook-house. The one latrine yet made was a hole dug into the side of the support trench. In short, there was as much to be done to make the place habitable as defendable.

The day passed slowly, with the sun doing its best to cheer the bruised landscape, won at the cost of so many thousands of lives, which we could see stretching away for miles behind us. Below in the valley ran Dewdrop Trench with its piles of dead. Beyond it the ground climbed slightly to where the remains of Lesbœufs Wood poked jagged, splintered fingers at the sky. Somewhere to the left was Sailly Saillisel, and to the right Ginchy and Morval. What a view it was ! Yet, for all its spaciousness, there was nothing to see, just mile upon mile of emptiness, with never a house or a tree, a hedge or a spot of green to break the absolute monotony of tint and feature. Here and there, as if by magic, arose black spouts, marking the explosions of shells, and passing clouds cast purple shadows on the dun. Otherwise, all was drab and formless, as one imagines Earth must have been before the appearance of life.

How I wished, as often during the war years, that I was painter enough to be able faithfully to record the scene on canvas, sparing nothing and missing nothing. I longed for this power, not with any idea of holding a mirror up to the futility of

war, but to show the talkers, the preachers, and the
shirkers at home what they were missing, and how
little they could ever understand of our feelings,
our hopes, or our fears. I realised only too clearly
that those in England would never know what
things were like, nor could descriptions, however
eloquent, convey any true picture. Nature was
strangely jealous of her scars, which she was quick
to cover from all who were not actually present
when they were inflicted.

I had the same longing each time I came home
on leave and saw Kent hop-fields or Hampshire
meadows green and trim and quiet, but with this
difference—I wanted to depict them, because in
those sudden wonderful views from the windows
of the railway carriage I was discovering the beauty
and peace of England, whereas I wanted to show
the void of war, to which I was habituated, to those
who knew it not.

I had barely got back to Company Headquarters
before we were provided with an aerial thrill.
Two German aeroplanes flew over at a great height.
" Archie " got on to them at once and surprisingly
enough scored a direct hit with the fourth or fifth
shell.   There was a little puff of orange smoke
against the blue, and a white wing with its black
cross came fluttering down like a wounded butter-
fly.   We applauded such accurate shooting with
never a thought for the pilot so suddenly hurled to
death.

Quickly the short winter day drew to its close,
and with the coming of dusk the front woke to
activity.   Shells from both sides began to swish
hurriedly overhead, bursting in dim fountains of

sparks far in front or away in rear ; machine guns
searched angrily for the movement that would
start with the dark. On all sides Verey lights
hissed and wavered in the sky, while from the
shell-holes in front the enemy kept firing up lights
of different colours, apparently as signals.

By now, I thought, the Battalion would be
parading after an early tea in Camp 34, and I
rejoiced secretly that I was ensconced in the earth
close to the enemy instead of starting out on that
weary journey to the line at the head of a company
of men, burdened with heavy equipment, harassed
by shell-fire, sliding and slithering in and out of
shell-holes and old trenches, each man straining his
whole energy in keeping in sight the vague blur
of the man in front, all ultimately following blindly
a guide who had only the haziest notion of his
whereabouts. I could almost hear the constantly
reiterated shout of " Halt in front ! Halt in
front ! Man stuck," as some poor devil sank up
to the waist in an unseen hole. I could feel the
awful tenseness as the line waited till he had been
hauled out. I could picture the guide, giving way
to an uneasiness which forced itself upon him,
come to a standstill and peer anxiously about him,
whereupon the line of men, their eyes over-strained
in piercing the darkness, would telescope one on
top of the other and, fluently indignant, jostle the
guide into moving on somewhere, anywhere, that
he might not, by standing still, add to the existing
hopelessness the crowning despair of " being lost."

As it happened, the company reached the Devons'
Headquarters in the sunken road without casualties.
Then started the worst part of the journey, that

half-mile through the valley where my guide had told me " it was easy to go wrong at night." Luckily enough, the company struck the white tape which had been laid by some enterprising engineer, and many a silent prayer must have gone up for that unknown benefactor from those who followed its slender guidance. Grim though that valley had appeared in the early morning light, it was terrible in the darkness. The atmosphere was significant enough to inspire even the most stolid with respectful haste. It was not altogether the dead, whom the hurrying eye noted, unconsciously, sprawling in the grotesque attitudes in which they had fallen ; nor yet the impressively new shell-holes which the accustomed nose registered immediately by the pungent reek of fresh lyddite. It was not altogether the sudden flaring glow of the Very lights, suspiciously vigilant over No-Man's-Land ; nor yet the staccato bark of an occasional machine-gun startling the crowded stillness, its unnaturally bold rat-tat-tat stealing hastily away in stealthy listening echoes into the silence which closed in more heavily oppressive than before. It was some of these things and all of them. The night was dark, so dark that a man was invisible at a few yards' distance, and yet for all their haste men crouched low along the tape as though they felt a hundred baleful eyes to be upon them. In that valley, deserted but for their own presence, and yet filled with a nameless dread, men had a vividly stifling sense of unbearable crowding.

The passage of the valley was accomplished with only two casualties. One of these was Sergeant Chamberlain, who was acting Company Sergeant-

Major in place of Scott. He did not hold the post for long, poor devil. The company were struggling up towards the line with the Devon guide first, Mac second, and Chamberlain third. As they topped a small rise, Mac, who was wearing a light-coloured leather jerkin, stepped aside to turn it inside out so as to minimise any risk of detection by the enemy. No sooner had he done so than a random whizz-bang thudded into the ground on the very spot where he had stood, exploding in the mud with a smothered burst. The sergeant rose bodily : fell back dead, killed by concussion. It says much for Mac that, despite his own wonderful escape, he had taken the papers from the body and moved the line off again before the last man had time to close up and learn the meaning of the temporary stoppage.

Meanwhile the Devons had been getting more and more impatient to get out. Hour succeeded hour and still no sign of the relieving company came to us waiting in the trench, until at about 11 p.m. there was a sound of trudging feet and the clank of metal, and Mac's voice hailed us out of the gloom. The journey had taken them seven hours !

There followed much jostling, scrambling, and cursing ; men floundering in the mud, officers and N.C.O.'s wrestling with the farce of handing over receipts for stores and ammunition which they could not see, much less count ; until at last the Devons were all clear and we had taken over the sector.

Before the Devon's Headquarters moved off, C.S.M. Radford (whom I then met for the first time, but who was destined to become a firm friend during the next eighteen months before being taken prisoner on the Aisne in 1918) handed over to my servant Briggs a half-full jar of rum. Generosity of such a kind was so rare as to be worth remarking, and is an indication of the existing determination not to carry out of the line anything that could be left behind.

As for our dispositions, Mac and George passed on with Nos. 5 and 6 platoons to the front line, No. 7 platoon, under Corporal Robinson, remained around Company Headquarters in the support line, and No. 8 went into the protecting T-head out of the communication trench.

It was now my job to go round the company to tell all and sundry what the place looked like in daylight and what they had to do. No sooner had I arrived in the front line than the first casualty occurred, a new recruit being shot in the mouth by a stray bullet. He was bleeding freely, but did not seem seriously hurt, and after the stretcher-bearers had patched him up as best they could in the darkness, he was sent down with an orderly to the M.O. at Battalion Headquarters.

Getting Mac and George together, I explained the position to them. I told them that it looked as if we had a stiff job ahead of us. To begin with, the mud made communications so difficult that some delegation of responsibility was necessary. Although Company Headquarters were less than 100 yards from Fall Trench, the distance measured in terms of mud was so great that I could not be sure of maintaining any effective touch from the support line. I told Mac, therefore, that he would have to take charge of the front-line trench. Secondly, it would be necessary to find out who were our nearest neighbours on the right flank, and to establish contact with them. It was agreed that No. 8 platoon were best placed to do this, and that they should send out a patrol of one N.C.O. and two men without delay.

But by far the most important task was somehow or other to put the rudimentary trenches into something approaching a defensive system before daylight. Accordingly I told Mac that his first job must be to see that a sap was dug out so as to secure a view into the dead ground in front. Lastly, but not least, I impressed upon him—and indeed upon every man I passed—that as there were no dug-outs our safety depended upon our energy in digging, as a deep, narrow trench was as safe from shell-fire as anything but a tunnel or mined dug-out ; further, that since we did not know where the Germans were, it was unlikely that they were any the wiser as to our whereabouts. The order, therefore, was " dig like blazes all night and lie doggo all day "—hard orders to have to give to men, many of them strangers to the regiment, whose period of rest had been exhausting discomfort, and who were now utterly weary after their seven hours' tramp through mud and débris in the dark. Which was why I tried to explain things personally to every individual.

The response was wonderful, as may be judged from the following incident :

Before I had started from Company Headquarters I had put the same facts before Corporal Robinson. Now Robinson, No. 8300, a New Zealander and a regular soldier of some twelve years' service, rejoiced in the nickname of " Buggy," which is to imply that he was not " all there." The sobriquet was earned, I had been informed, because of certain eccentricities, as, for example, his habit on frosty mornings in the breastworks at Laventie, during the winter of 1914–15, of suddenly restoring his circulation by running violently down the trench puffing hard, " Shoo ! Shoo ! Look out ! I'm an express train." He was also said to have solved the problem of providing scrambled eggs in the line by breaking a dozen fresh eggs or so into his water bottle and pouring them out as required ! Eccentricities he may have had, but no more resourceful soldier ever served. He was an especial source of pride to me, since when I had taken over the company he was one of its black sheep, always in trouble. His years of service had automatically won him a lance stripe long before, but he had had it taken from him for some drunken scrape. I was at once impressed with his intelligence and resource, and probably more from a lucky inspiration than any reasoning, I decided that what he wanted was to be given responsibility, and that his unsatisfactory conduct sprang from his being a seasoned private soldier under non-commissioned officers, the majority of whom were raw and inexperienced boys. Against the Colonel's advice, I carried my point, and was richly rewarded by seeing Robinson change in the twinkling of an eye into a most valuable N.C.O. He was a most lovable character, and his death outside the ramparts at Ypres, in 1917, left a gap in the ranks of the regiment that was never filled.

But to return. When I had left Company Headquarters it had been in a trench about four and a
half feet deep. When I returned it was nearer
seven feet ! Robinson's platoon—mostly miners—
had excelled themselves, and if the trench was only
less than two feet wide at the bottom, it was now
safe against anything but the biggest howitzer shell.

Worn-out after being " on the go " continuously
for sixteen hours, I sat down, with a sigh of relief
and a pull at my flask, to write my report and
draw a sketch map of my dispositions by the
jealously guarded light of a stub of candle. I had
barely begun when there was a scream, a flash, and
a thud close at hand. Out went the candle, and
some one down the trench cried, " Stretcher-
bearers ! Stretcher-bearers ! " Our two stretcher-
bearers, Hammond and Pettican, the one from
Tyneside, the other from Colchester, hurried past
me, and as I relit my candle I heard the following
dialogue :

Low groans of " I'm 'it ! I'm 'it ! " followed
by a pause.

Then from one of the stretcher-bearers, " Nay,
Bob, you're not hit."

" I'm 'it, I'm 'it, I'm 'it ! " groans getting louder.

Another pause. Then, " Nay, Bob, you're not
hit at all."

" I'm 'it ! "—this time in a positive roar—" I
am 'it, I tell thee, and a bloody big soss and all
on top o' t' head ! "

Followed a gust of laughter, and eventually the
explanation that the stricken one was Private
Robert Parkin, forty-two years of age, toothless,
and from Rotherham ; that he had been perched

up on the high fire-step as sentry when the shell
arrived some five yards in front of him ; that the
said shell had burst in the mud and blown a large
clod at him, hitting him on the helmet, knocking
him down all the way to the bottom of the trench
and all the wind out of his body. Never was man
more certain that he was mortally wounded !

It should here be interpolated that Parkin was
one of the few people who preferred the coverless
ditches of the Somme to the more highly organised
trenches farther north, for the sole reason that they
were free of rats. He had a rooted dread of rats.
Night after night in the sector from the Brickstacks
at Cuincy to the Quarries at Hulluch, no matter
what time I came back to the dug-out, I was sure to
find Parkin sitting nodding in a corner, the inevitable cigarette in his toothless gums, instead of sleeping. " It's them rats, sir," he would explain. " I
can't abide them. I hate them much worse than I
do Johnny Squarehead across the way."   Like
many a British soldier he had no personal dislike
of the enemy. Indeed, Parkin was only a soldier
by accident, since he had, on his own confession,
joined up in a moment of alcoholic exuberance
after seeing a friend off to the front. He never
remembered taking the shilling, and " when the
sergeant come and claimed " him next morning he
was as surprised as his wife was annoyed. But he
stayed in France to the bitter end and, escaping
all injury, became my servant after Briggs was
missing in May 1918, and eventually was one of
those who helped to carry my kit off the troopship
Huntzend which brought us back to be demobilised
in February 1919.

All this is by the way. I went on with my
writing. So far as our immediate front was concerned, "conditions were quiet." From time to
time there was the deep drone of a heavy shell
lumbering overhead ; the muffled report of its
distant burst. Now and then a whizz-bang would
stab the darkness with its vicious hiss and flash.
Rifle-fire crackled and popped, and at intervals the
harsh rattle of machine-guns sounded up and down
the front. But around me the only noises were the
clink of spade and pick, and the grunts of digging
men.

"Things are quiet," I wrote, "and work is
proceeding as well as the mud will allow. There
is nothing to report."

Yet tragedy was abroad little more than a hundred
yards from me.

A prompt start had been made on digging out
the two saps, and to protect those engaged on the
task Skett had sent out a covering party under a
2nd Lieutenant named Pym, just as I had sent out
one under Mac. Pym, who was yet another importation from the ranks of the Canadian forces,
had barely got his party out in front when a German
machine-gun opened fire. Every man threw himself flat, but it was only a random burst. Although
from some shell-hole close to them in the darkness
Pym ordered his men back to the trench, he himself
did not return with them. Neither did he follow
them in. He was a wild individual, so that at first
his absence was not out of the ordinary. Then
Skett called out to him by name. There was no
reply. Alarmed, Skett, having no other officer
with him except the other subaltern in charge of the

isolated post on the left, sent out a first and then a second patrol in charge of a non-commissioned officer. These scoured the inky waste, crawling from shell-hole to shell-hole, calling the missing officer's name. All in vain. Poor Skett was at his wits' end. The first time he had been in charge of a company in the front line, and here was one of his officers missing. Pym might have been captured, possibly killed, but he might equally well be lying wounded or dying in No-Man's-Land.

Getting together a larger patrol, Skett sent them out in charge of a trusted sergeant, and stumbled along Fall Trench to explain the situation to Mac. The two agreed that if this last patrol met with no success it was essential that an officer's party should go out. Skett had no officer to send, while orders were insistent and explicit that company commanders were not to leave the line themselves. Mac immediately volunteered to go himself as soon as he could get permission from me to leave his sap, and sent off a note to me.

The messenger plodded down the communication trench to Company Headquarters where, after sending my report to the Adjutant, I was trying to get a little sleep on the floor of the trench. " Work on sap going well," I read. " Can I go to A Company and have a look for Pym ? " " Have a look for Pym ? " I thought. " What the devil does he want to do that for ? " I knew they were friends and that it was their habit to forgather for a talk and a smoke when work was slack. " Blast Mac ! " I said to myself. " Can't he understand that we have *got* to get these trenches a decent depth before daylight ? " and promptly wrote a reply to the effect that this was " no time for demonstrations of affection," and that he was to carry on with the sap till it was finished before indulging in any informal trench conference.

In other words, even at such a short distance from the scene no word had reached me, nor had Mac, thinking I already knew, made it clear that any untoward incident had occurred. Of course, as soon as he got my reply, Mac realised what had happened, hastily wrote another note, and went back to his sap to wait for the few minutes it would take me to come up as soon as I knew the situation.

Meanwhile, Skett returning to his own company, had found that the third patrol had just crawled in to report that they had found no trace of Pym. Desperate, as time was of the utmost importance, Skett determined to go himself, against orders though this was. He conceived it to be his personal responsibility to leave no stone unturned to find Pym. Some premonition must have come to him, for as he collected a few reliable men together to go with him, he turned to his servant, and handing him the valuables and documents out of his pockets said, " Here are the wages I owe you. You'd better take them while you can get them," and without more ado scrambled out of the trench.

Hardly had he put a foot in No-Man's-Land than he fell back dead, his head split open by a random bullet. Who shall say that he did not know his fate was upon him ? Those who had been with him from the morning have little doubt about it.

This was the news that greeted me as I reached Mac in response to his second note. A Company being now without an officer, I took over the

company and at once sent out patrols under both
Mac and George.   All night these two scoured
the ground in front, but no trace was found, nor has
word ever since been heard of Pym.

The mud had swallowed him up as completely
as it had, by delaying communication between Mac
and myself, killed poor Skett.   Him we buried
before daylight as reverently as we could in the
circumstances, digging a grave between bursts of
machine-gun fire in the parados of Fall Trench.

III

TRENCH-HOLDING

III

TRENCH-HOLDING

Dawn on the 11th found us all feeling the effects of our labours and the lack of sleep. Legs were attacked by acute shooting pains due to the strain of constant movement in the mud. Eyes smarted with tiredness. Faces and fingernails were caked with mud.

Directly stand-to was over, the majority of the men fell straight down to sleep, but for Mac and me there was little rest, as the Colonel arrived and insisted on walking the whole weary way round both company fronts ! He approved my dispositions and told me he had decided to leave me in charge of both companies, but to send up another subaltern to do duty with A Company.

As soon as he had gone I sat myself down to breakfast, and if in after years those of us who survive are afflicted with chronic indigestion, we shall have ample excuse. The difficulty of cooking without detection by the enemy, and the unpleasantness of the petrol-impregnated water led me to eschew tea. Instead, I made a hearty meal of " Maconochie "—a tinned form of stew with meat and vegetables—eaten cold and washed down with a tea-cup full of rum.

The day again turned out bright and sunny, and the craving for sleep passed off. This was just as

well, for Cropper, the additional subaltern, reported for duty and had to be taken round to
A Company and duly installed. Our night's digging
had been most successful throughout, and as I
wandered up to see Mac, I found I had hardly to
stoop in the communication trench, while Fall
Trench was now quite a respectable line.

I found Mac distinctly ill-at-ease. Almost at
once he supplied the explanation by asking if I
would give him permission to go out and hunt
among the dead lying around Dewdrop Trench
for the body of his brother, who had been reported
" missing, believed killed " in an attack near
Lesbœufs some three weeks earlier. Apparently
Mac had just learned that some of the corpses in
the valley belonged to units of his brother's division,
and he was impatient to be off at once on his morbid
search. I refused point-blank to allow him to go,
not from any military reason but simply because,
as I tried to show him, it could do no good. It
was almost unthinkable that he would ever find his
brother, and even if he did do so, the body would
probably be so mangled or decomposed that the
discovery would only leave a dreadful blot on his
memory. After a little while he saw the force of
my argument, and cheered up, and I spent a great
part of the morning with him, making a thorough
examination of the ground in front. The horizon
was the line of the Bapaume Road, many of the
poplars along which were still intact. The middle
distance was as featureless as the ground in rear,
save where on a slope a tumbled outline of masonry
was recognisable as Cemetery Circle, supposed to
be an enemy strong point. Certainly some move-

ment was to be seen there and, emboldened perhaps by the quiet which prevailed, I was foolish enough to stick head and shoulders over the top to point out the spot to the machine-gun crew as a suitable one for their attention. A deafening clop! sounded in my right ear, and I fell off the fire-step, realising that that sniper's aim must have been very accurate, otherwise the bullet would not have sounded so loudly.

Wandering round our little sector, talking here with some Yorkshire corporal, here with some of the new draft, the morning passed easily and pleasantly, to be rounded off with the midday meal, chiefly bully and a little whisky diluted with the precious pure water in my water-bottle.

Shortly afterwards a very hot and breathless artillery officer and his orderly fell into our head-quarters trench, dragging their telephone wire with them. They were representatives of a 6-inch gun battery which was proposing that afternoon to shell a piece of trench which was said to lie opposite the front of A Company, and to be still manned by the enemy. This fragment was all that remained of Zenith Trench which, with the help of the mud, had resisted the " full dress " attack which had cost us so heavily last time we had been in line, and the officer's attitude suggested that he was apologising on behalf of the Royal Regiment for having been so remiss as to leave even so short a length of enemy trench undemolished. I was not disposed very charitably towards him, as so far we had gone almost unmolested, and experience had taught us that any form of artillery offensiveness promptly evoked retaliation, which as often as not fell on

the P.B.I.   Still, I extended to him the ordinary
courtesies of the trenches in the shape of a cigarette
and whisky and water in a tin cup, and then escorted
him to A Company's front line, where Cropper
joined us.   By careful scrutiny of No-Man's-Land
we managed to identify something which we took
to be the surviving stretch of trench, though we
were by no means certain until the battery started
firing.   Then as our Forward Observing Officer
corrected the range, and the shells started falling
all round the spot, first one and then another
German, ludicrous in their coal-scuttle helmets,
long coats and boots, emerged and floundered
wildly into the nearest deep shell-hole.   Cropper,
seizing a rifle, at once opened fire and continued
firing, with a man loading a spare rifle for him.

There must have been twenty or thirty Germans
who bolted, but Cropper's fire was not accurate
enough to account for more than four or five at
most, though we could not really tell which were
hit or which had merely stumbled and fallen.   Still,
it was some consolation to know that those who
were not casualties must have been severely fright-
ened !   Their " shoot " over, our gunner guests
took a speedy departure, while we waited appre-
hensively for the retaliation which, for some un-
accountable reason, came not.

As dusk was gathering I went back by way of
the front line so that I could see the company at
stand-to, chatted to Mac and George, and spent
some time with the officerless No. 8 platoon in the
T-head.   The men were very cheerful.   The patrol
they had sent out during the night had established
that our nearest neighbours on the right were men

of the Royal Irish (now Ulster) Rifles, in isolated posts some two hundred yards away. During the day the platoon had been resting, and mention of sleep reminded me that I had had none for a very strenuous forty-eight hours, and I promised myself that I would " get down to it " as soon as I got back to Company Headquarters and had got off my night's report.

It was quite dark by the time I did get back, and Robinson came up and asked me in a confidential undertone if he might go and " hunt for souvenirs " behind the line. He was an incorrigible " scrounger," for ever collecting the flotsam of battle—shell nose-caps, German grenades, cap rosettes, weapons, even gloves and boots—which he would take back and sell to the Army Service Corps, and I recognised his request as a polite way of saying that he wished to go out and loot the enemy dead lying between us and Dewdrop Trench. He and his platoon had done such excellent work and he was such a law unto himself that I had no heart to refuse him, although I could not give him permission to leave the trench. I compromised by saying that I should know nothing about it. If he went and returned without being found by any one in authority or hit by the enemy, all would be well. If he were caught, then he'd have to stand the racket ! I further told him that he must search every British corpse and bring me back the pay-books, after which what he did with the Germans was no concern of mine.

He hopped over the parados without more ado and was lost in the gloom. Not long afterwards the ration party arrived panting and sweating with their heavy loads of sand-bags full of bread, bully, jam, and biscuits, and petrol-tins of water. They reported two of their number hit on the way from Battalion Headquarters and their loads lost in the darkness. Luckily that most precious item of the day's rations—the half-jar of rum—had not been lost !

The rations carriers' was a most unenviable task, as thankless as it was dangerous. Rarely in those days did they complete their double journey without casualties. Occasionally the whole party was wiped out while their company waited, parched and famished, for the water and food scattered about the mud and shell-holes. Water was more precious even than victuals. It was everywhere "but not a drop to drink," while the full petrol-tins were cruel burdens to shoulder over a mile or so of battle-field.

With the day's duties successfully accomplished and the enemy contenting himself with shelling of a desultory nature and mostly directed far away in rear, I curled myself up on the trench floor and was soon off to sleep. Hardly had my senses left me than I was up and on edge in a second ! Shells had begun to fall more quickly all around us ! Then, with a whoosh of metal overhead, down came the barrage ! Explosions whirled, stamped, and pounded the tortured ground ; the splitting hiss and bang of the field guns screaming above the deep, earth-shaking thud ! thud ! of the heavies until they blended into the one steady pandemonium of drumfire. The trenches rocked and trembled, while their garrisons, blinded by the flashes, choked by the acrid fumes, pressed themselves tight to the

sodden walls as the avalanche of metal roared above
and around them.

Out of the smoke along the trench emerged a
runner, crouching low. " Front line — Verey
lights—urgent ! " he croaked, his tongue parched
with the biting smoke. " Verey lights ! " I yelled,
" Where are they ? " They should have come up
with the rations, but none had arrived. " There
are some Boche ones here, sir," shouted a voice I
recognised as belonging to Purkiss, the company
cook. " Are you sure they are white ones ? " I
roared back across the din. " Yes, sir," was the
assurance, " Parkin fired one off in the latrine this
morning and it burnt white all right ! " Seizing
the rotting box marked " Signal Patronen," Mac's
messenger departed again into the smoke. By now
the explosions around us were fewer, but the curtain
of fire, leaping and crashing, hung relentlessly in
the valley, which raged and seethed, an inferno of
smoke and destruction.

So the Boche had done what we feared ! He
had dropped his barrage in rear of us to cut off
supports while he came across and " snaffled " my
two companies ! This was the conviction which
possessed me.

" Stand-to, No. 7 ! " I shouted, at the same time
sending off one runner to order A Company to do
the same, and another to Mac for news. While
behind us the barrage flared and thundered, in front
all was quiet. As we stood, tense and alert, peering
over the parapet, all we could see was the black
crest of the ridge some fifteen yards in front over
which rose, wavered, and fell the enemy Verey
lights, some burning white and steady, others

soaring up in a fountain of golden sparks. Over
our heads the rush of shells continued, but from in
front there came no rattle of small arms. Clearly
the enemy had not yet attacked.

Suddenly, from about the position of Fall Trench,
over the brow there was a hiss, and up flew a
rocket. Horror of horrors ! It burst with a rosy
glow and hung, a ball of claret light, over our line !
Before it had died out a second went up, bursting
this time into golden rain. That German box of
lights had been a mixed lot for signal purposes !
But what had we done ? Whatever request to the
enemy had we in our extremity sent up ? For a
few breathless minutes we waited, momentarily
expecting the barrage to be shortened and fall on
our unlucky heads.

Instead, just as a thunder-shower abruptly ends,
so the shelling on the instant died away, as suddenly
as it had begun, and only a few random shells, like
scattered raindrops, burst sporadically in rear before
silence, heavy and oppressive, succeeded strife.

All danger of an attack over, I stood the men
down and hurried off to the front line where Mac
laughingly described what a shock he had got when
he sent up the two German lights. We thought
over what signals they might be, and, after much
fruitless conjecture over the first claret affair, we
decided that the golden rain rocket must mean
" Lengthen range : we are here," as whenever the
enemy started shelling a forest of golden rockets
would rise from the shell-holes in front. That we
were right was soon confirmed, and the Divisional
Intelligence Report next day contained the reassuring information that " hostile signal golden

rocket bursting into golden rain means lengthen range instead of barrage." Much more important from our point of view was the fact that never again until we were relieved did a German shell fall on our company front ! Even more wonderful to relate, neither A nor B Company had a single man hit during the enemy's shelling, which we could only put down to a belated retaliation for our " shoot " of the afternoon.

My return to Company Headquarters coincided with the reappearance of Robinson. One look at his drawn and ashen face showed me that, tough old hand as he was, he had had a fright, realising which, I forbore to curse him as I meant to, and merely asked him what had happened. His reply was that after he left the support line he turned down towards Dewdrop Trench, and that as he was examining some very promising bodies he had been caught by the barrage and forced to spend a very unpleasant and smelly half-hour in the same shell-hole with " two dead Jerries." Then he had tried to get back to the trench, but losing his way had roamed and groped about in the filth and darkness until he had been challenged by Mac's men in Fall Trench ! In other words, he had passed through the big gap on our right flank and had had a very narrow escape from walking unwittingly into the German lines. It was a very chastened " Buggy " that rejoined his platoon.

As for me, I had had about enough, and I lay down once again at the bottom of the narrow trench, where there was just room for my body, and slept the sleep of exhaustion till aroused, numb and cramped, for stand-to four hours later. This was the first proper rest I had had since I had left Camp 34.

I got up to Fall Trench just as the men were standing-to, yawning and stretching themselves as they manned the fire-step, and, passing down the trench without seeing Mac, I asked one of his platoon where he was. " He's issuing rum to the covering party, sir ! " was the reply. And so it was. It appeared that when he had reached the last man digging in the point of the sap the thought had occurred to him that the covering party must be cold and stiff lying out in the mud in front. In procession, though not quite erect, Mac, followed by Sergeant Priestley with the rum-jar, and a private bearing the ceremonial cigarette tin, had walked out to the party in No-Man's-Land and solemnly issued rum in the shell-hole. The value of such apparently dare-devil gestures was evident from the fact that the news had travelled with chuckles down the sap and into the trench long before the three had got safely back again.

What a typical November morning that was ! Dawn stole upon us swathed in shrouds of swirling mist, shutting us in still further upon ourselves, surrounding us with its impenetrable curtain. The cold dank air was heavy with the smell of decay. Objects were invisible at six paces, still invisibility was safety, so after stand-down we all took the opportunity of getting on top of the trenches and having a look round.

It was a relief to stretch one's legs and straighten one's back for a while. Between the trenches, we found, were only enemy dead, here a field-grey arm poked out of a shell-hole, there a heavy boot ; here a man lay, head on crooked arm, as if asleep ; there the remains of three or four littered the crater made by the shell that had killed them. Beside the communication trench a huge German lay sprawled on his back, arms and legs splayed starfish-like, sightless eyes gazing perplexedly heavenward. So that, I noted, was the cause of the aroma which I always encountered on my way to the front line, but which did not prevent one of the men going busily through the corpse's pockets and discovering a small piccolo which he presented to me as a memento ! This generosity on the part of the finder, I should explain, sprang from disappointment. What all the men were after really was the Iron Cross, the dream of every souvenir-hunter, and which, were the lucky finder mercenary enough to wish to dispose of it, commanded a very good market.

We found also ample proof that, blown out of his last trenches in the battle zone, the enemy had resorted to a system of fortified shell-holes. A big crater would be chosen, deepened for safety and a step dug for fire-purposes. Into it would be put, we judged, two or three men, a machine gun, a Verey pistol and a plentiful supply of ammunition, lights, and " iron rations " and brandy or schnapps. To cover them, we found they had large ground sheets which could be stretched over the hole, thus converting it into something reasonably habitable. There were two or three of these fortified craters between the trenches, and out of them we took many parcels of signal lights, some tins of German bully marked " Rindfleisch "—which the men swore was human flesh in tins !—and two or three hinged iron boxes, designed to carry machine-gun belts.

While we were still eagerly hunting about " on the top," word was brought me that the Colonel was on his way to the line with the Brigadier, news which caused every one to be packed off to his station at once. I hurried up to the front line, warning Mac and Cropper as I passed them, and arriving on the left of A Company in time to salute the C.O. With him was Brigadier-General Fagan, who had only recently taken over command of the brigade and who was not destined to hold his command for long—which was a pity, as he was a keen soldier, always determined to see for himself, no matter how bad the conditions. As we were situated none of us would have been surprised if the Colonel had satisfied himself with coming up to the line once, but he came up every day, and the Brigadier himself once—a small point, perhaps, but one which was not missed by a single man, as their comments showed. But what none of us knew at the time was that the Colonel's daily visit to his companies took him no fewer than four hour's strenuous walking ! How long it took the Brigadier to come up from still farther in rear can only be conjectured, but the very fact that he would thereby be absent from his headquarters for many hours should be some answer to those who demand to know why general officers did not put in more frequent appearances in the front line.

Obviously the General was surprised and gratified to find the beginnings of a really sound trench system where, as he admitted, he had expected only a chain of posts scattered in a line of linked shell-holes. And Fall Trench, now complete with two saps from which a full view could be had of the gully in front, certainly did return us a reward for our labours. Cleared of mud, fire-stepped, deep, and continuous along the two-company front, it looked most efficient, but I modestly explained that we had been lucky in the weather, and that if it had rained much no amount of work could have achieved the result. Most of all was I proud of the men. Their spirits had been magnificent. They had worked like niggers, with never a shirker amongst them, and as the General went round even his practised eye was slow to find a fault in their bearing, their alertness, or the cleanness of their arms. Rifles were well-cared for, and well-oiled bombs were stacked in neat piles on the fire-step near each sentry post. Moreover, thanks to Mac and George, the sentries knew their jobs and the lie of the land in front.

At no other time in the war did I meet a better, keener, or more reliable set of men than that mixed Yorkshire-Northumbrian contingent in front of Le Transloy. With little except cold bully to eat, with less water to drink, and none to wash in, with nowhere to sleep except the open trench, they behaved for the three days as if the whole affair were some tiresome form of entertainment which they were compelled to sit through.

The pacifist may inveigh against war's hideousness, leagues and societies may condemn it in vigorous resolutions and solemnly declare that " there must be no more war," yet the fact remains that, terrifying as they sometimes, and uncomfortable as they often were, the war years will stand out in the memories of vast numbers of those who fought as the happiest period of their lives. And the clue to this perhaps astonishing fact is that though the war may have let loose the worst it also brought out the finest qualities in men.

In spite of all differences in rank, we were comrades, brothers, dwelling together in unity. We were privileged to see in each other that inner, ennobled self which in the grim, commercial struggle of peace-time is all too frequently atrophied for lack of opportunity of expression. We could note the intense affection of soldiers for certain officers, their absolute trust in them. We saw the love passing the love of women of one " pal " for his " half-section." We saw in his letters home which came to us for censoring, the filial devotion of the " toughest," drunkenest private for his aged mother back in the slums by the Tyne at North Shields. We saw the indomitable kindliness of the British character expressing itself towards the French children, the wretched mangy French dogs, and, yes, even to the German wounded and prisoners ! The English soldier could not hate his enemies for long. Only a few days previously during the attack on Zenith Trench, when, with a third of the battalion killed or wounded, the shivering remainder stayed two days on the scene of the action, in rudimentary water-logged trenches under incessant rain and steady shell-fire : rations could not be got up, yet, wet, famished, and miserable as they were, the men insisted on sharing their infrequent mugs of tea with a wounded German, who, hit in the side, lay under a sopping oilskin in the trench. " Here's a drop of tea for Fritz," the men would say, as they propped up the captive and fed him as a nurse would feed a patient.

We were privileged, in short, to see a reign of goodwill among men, which the piping times of peace, with all their organised charity, their free meals, free hospitals, and Sunday sermons have never equalled. Despite all the propaganda for Christian fellowship and international peace, there is more animosity, uncharitableness, and lack of fellowship in one business office now than in a brigade of infantry in France then. Otherwise, we could never have stood the strain.

But this is to digress !

Before leaving, the Brigadier had some very encouraging things to say about the way we had organised our little sector, and from the Colonel we learnt that despite the weight of metal which had been hurled at them during the night, C and D Companies also had escaped without casualties, which was a striking exemplification of the enormous number of projectiles necessary to destroy one human life, and of the utterly incomprehensible manner in which a trench could be hammered and blown out of all recognition by shell-fire without a man in it being hit. Conversation delayed their departure so long that the mist had begun to clear before the General, the Colonel, and their orderlies had scrambled over the parados and started with as much haste as was consonant with dignity to get across the danger zone between us and the Sunken Road. By the time I had plodded back to Company Headquarters the sun had broken through with the welcome assurance of another fine day.

There are those who deny that breakfast is, as its name implies, the most important meal of the day, but in the trenches no one could question it for a moment. No matter how violent, sulphurous, or bloody the night, no matter how tense the grim ceremonial of " stand-to " which ushered in the day, the command " stand-down " was almost invariably followed by a lull along the whole front. Hostilities were temporarily suspended by mutual, if mute, consent, and for what reason except that after the strained hours of darkness English and German alike turned with relaxation to break their fast ? For anything from an hour to two hours the most vicious noise to be heard in the trench was the sizzling of frying bacon. Then some machine-gunner, cheerful from his meal, would break the spell with the " Pop-pop-op-pop-pop ! " call on his Vickers, which never failed to evoke the slower " pop-pop " from some heavy machine-gun within the German lines.

There was something very refreshing about this breakfast truce. Above all, is it associated in my mind with a brief triumph of the kindly smells of Nature over those more sinister ones of man's making. For a few minutes the sun and dew distilled a faint fragrance even from the freshly turned earth or the coarse weeds bruised by the night's shelling, before the moisture evaporated and allowed the normal odours of trench life to assert themselves. Even then the all-pervading reek of chlorate of lime would be overcome for a while by the homely acrid smell of the cook's wood fire, and—oh, most welcome !—of bacon.

But as I reached my headquarters my nose registered none of these things. No. 7 platoon were starting the day as each man, except the sentry on the high fire-step, thought best. Some were asleep, others busy with their breakfast. What miserable breakfasts we were compelled to during those four days ! Bread, whiskery with strands of sand-bag, butter, and a dollop of cold " Maconochie " or bully beef, washed down, if we were lucky, with a half-cupful of neat rum. Tea was even harder to go without than bacon, but it was impossible to light a fire during daylight without giving the enemy gunners a fresh target. Lunch, tea, and dinner were repetitions of breakfast, except that at nightfall the old-soldier's ingenuity triumphed over circum-stances. " Buggy " Robinson contrived a kind of oven in the side of the trench, covering the hole with a ground-sheet pegged into the earth with rifle cartridges. Inside he put his stove, made of a tin of whale-oil—" trench feet, for the prevention of," to use the language of the period—soaked in which was a piece of " four-by-two " rifle rag. The heat given out was not very intense, but was enough to warm up one tin mug of liquid at a time, without any light showing in the trench. During the day Robinson improved his patent, and dug into the trench one of the salved German machine-gun belt boxes, which, with a lid that could be propped open, was most effective.

There was a good deal of laughter at breakfast over our various beards. Normally, officers and men alike shaved every day in the trenches—a regulation which the Colonel was very strict to have observed—but here it was quite impossible, with the result that some of us already sported very fair growths. Robinson had sprouted red, Parkin had a patchy fringe of grizzled stubble, but by common consent I won the prize with a really fearsome blackness which covered my entire face.

After every meal a wave of somnolence stole over me, which could only be thrown off by prompt action. Up I got, therefore, and trudged up to the front line for a chat. After a few minutes with No. 8 platoon in the T-head out of the communication trench, I moved on to Fall Trench. Mac was asleep, but George Hall was on duty and very angry with the brigade machine-gunners (the Machine-Gun Corps had not then been formed) because they would not fire. Together we interviewed the Corporal in charge of the section. His point was, quite rightly, that his gun was an extra defence to the trench system. If he fired it, he would risk giving away its position. Those were his orders. He should have to see his officer, etc. It was easy to see that George had rubbed him up the wrong way, but after a few jokes about the shells the Boches were sending over (I raised a hearty laugh by christening them " flying-commodes ! " How easy it was to make the men laugh if one was only sufficiently apposite and vulgar !) he was ready to fall in with any arrangements. Of course, there was actually little for him to fire at, but George's Lewis-gun team, who had been told off to keep an eye on Cemetery Circle, reported that they had again observed movement, and by peering cautiously over the top we could see that more fresh earth had been turned up. So both the Vickers and the Lewis gun were " laid " on the suspected area, and ordered to fire occasional bursts during the night.

Anything to make life unbearable for Brother Boche !

I noticed as I passed along that the trenches were not only beginning to look more efficient as defences, but more lived in, more " homely." German bayonets stuck in the walls served as pegs for bandoliers of cartridges, water bottles, and other parts of his complex harness which Mr. Atkins was accustomed to take off in the trenches. Here and there hung a gas-gong in the shape of a brass shell-case. The men could now not only stretch themselves on clean fire-steps for their sleep, a haversack or bag of Lewis-gun drums for pillow, but had begun to improvise all sorts of burrows and cubby-holes. Several, including Mac, had scooped a long, shallow grave into the front wall of the trench in which they could retire and lie full length like the recumbent effigy of some crusader in a church at home. In these niches they could rest undisturbed by people moving along the trench, and one or two men had secured greater privacy by hanging a ground-sheet over the hole. There was still no cookhouse, of course, but our conscientious sanitary N.C.O., Lance-Corporal Rumbold, had contrived two or three latrines as effective as they appeared hygienic.

Time slid by until lunch-time. You will observe that our periods were bounded by our meals. In this, as in many other things, there was a similarity between life in the line and on board ship. In both, one's area of action is restricted ; in both, one is cooped up for days together with the same people ; in both, there is little to keep mind and body interested except the prospect of the next meal. There were, it is true, certain dangers and annoyances in the trenches which are not tolerated on a pleasure cruise, but for all that the analogy is closer than at first appears.

After my midday meal the effect of the night's exertions could no longer be withstood, and rolling myself in a German ground-sheet, another piece of salvage of the morning, I laid myself down on the narrow floor of the trench for the second spell of sleep I had had since leaving camp. For two hours I slept dreamlessly and undisturbed until wakened by the cold which, striking upwards, had started aches and pains in my back and legs. It took me several minutes to thaw properly. This process was greatly assisted by a cup of " gun-fire " tea, that very brown, very sticky, but very stimulating beverage, brewed in Robinson's oven. If any one drink can be said to have won the war, the honour falls to " gun-fire " tea, technically teetotal though poisonous with tannin. Yet the apostles of temperance are so busy denying the value of alcohol and condemning the part it played in keeping us " alive and kicking," that they have not enscrolled a banner with the legend " Tea—1914–1918 " and flaunted it as they should before a forgetful nation's eyes !

One cup of that tea and a cigarette—a Woodbine for choice, procurable always from Parkin, who smoked nothing else—were guaranteed to put life into the weariest, and I was ready to sally forth again as the gathering dusk reminded me it was time for " stand-to."

Telling Robinson to stand his platoon to, I set off by way of A Company for a change, only to find that the support trench held the worst mud of all. The absence of rain seemed to have made it more viscous than ever, and I was hot and peevish by the time I had run Cropper to earth in the front line.

Cropper had been in the reserve battalion with me at Whitley Bay, where he had joined from Sandhurst in the autumn of 1915. We had come out together with the same draft to the 2nd Battalion, and together had suffered the miseries of Etaples and the Bull Ring. In a month's time he was to become my assistant adjutant, and afterwards succeed me in the adjutancy, only to be killed on the Somme in March 1918, not far from where we were that November night in 1916.

I found him, as I always picture him, completely unruffled. It was his first experience of command, but he tackled the job with the air of cheerful superiority which, springing from an inherent self-confidence surprising in one so young (he was then not more than twenty), stamped him as an exceptional leader.

The day had been quite uneventful so far as his company were concerned. " Hope it keeps quiet to-night," he added. It certainly was still. The artillery duel up north, in the direction of the Ancre, had subsided, and except for the lumbering of heavy shells passing high overhead from time to time like distant express trains, the only warlike sound was the occasional angry chorus of French 75's down by Sailly Saillisel.

We agreed that A Company's night's work should be to continue improving the sap and fire trench. B Company would do the same, while Mac took a patrol out to make a proper reconnaissance into the valley in front, so as to make sure it was clear of enemy residents, other than dead ones.

The men were standing-to as I walked down towards B Company. If this period of compulsory alertness for one hour at dusk and at dawn usually served no other useful purpose, it brought every one " on parade," as it were. It therefore afforded a good opportunity for officers to have an informal chat with this man and that, so that it took me some time to reach Mac. As I did so, a short burst of machine-gun fire sounded farther down the trench. "Listen!" said Mac, with a grin. "We've got the offensive spirit to-night all right!" following which he told me that he only wanted to take out one man with him on patrol—Sergeant Priestley, who had roamed a good many miles in No-Man's-Land with him before.

Corporal Robinson's first request to me on my return to headquarters was to be allowed to go out and resume the treasure hunt which had been so rudely interrupted the night previously. My reply was the same as before—that I would not see him go, and that he had to bring in the pay-books or other valuables of any British dead he might stumble across. With a very brisk, " Very good, sir! Thank you, sir!" he scrambled out of the trench and disappeared into the murk.

The ration party arrived with the Company Quartermaster-Sergeant. It was the event of the day. Here was touch with the outside world again; material, in the shape of food, drink, letters, and parcels from home; spiritual, in that there was some one fresh to talk to, who could pass on to us " military moles " the gossip which transport lines had gleaned from the whispering gallery of the back areas. Company Quartermaster-Sergeants were notoriously well-informed people. C.Q.M.S. Carlton was no exception. We were going to be relieved to-morrow night. Yes, we already knew that. Who were coming in ? The 1st Worcesters of our 24th Brigade. Was the division going to Italy ? Nothing known on this point, though it was said that we were to be withdrawn for a month's rest. Our visitor could only stay a few minutes, so my questions were fired at him, but he volunteered one interesting piece of information, that the night previously a German staff officer and his orderly had walked right through our lines, eventually fetching up at a ration dump where an enterprising Quartermaster made them prisoners before they could recover from their surprise. This incident shows at once the extraordinary disintegration of the front, and the ease with which one could get completely lost in that land made barren by artillery.

IV

RELIEF

IV

RELIEF

OUR relief by the 1st Battalion of the Worcester Regiment was confirmed in Battalion orders, and this piece of news, welcome in itself, was followed by a paragraph to the effect that the Brigadier had been much impressed with his visit to our front and wished to congratulate A and B Companies upon the work they had done, and " on the spirit displayed by all ranks." Secretly swelling with self-gratification, I read this out to No. 7 platoon, who received the news with a few very non-committal grunts, as if to say that the comments of visiting " brass-hats," whether congratulatory or censorious, left them cold. Undeterred, I sent off a runner to pass on the glad tidings to the other platoons, which I have no doubt were equally uninterested. Still, I convinced myself that as the credit ultimately belonged to the men, they ought to know that their good work had been noticed by those on Olympus.

The same runner who had brought the routine orders had also handed me a separate envelope, marked " Secret and Urgent," for which he required my signature as proof of receipt. I opened this to find that at 5.45 a.m. to-morrow (November 13) a large scale " Chinese attack " would take place on our front. In other words, our artillery were to open a heavy creeping barrage in order to delude the enemy into thinking that we were attacking, and thus to mask the real thrust which was to be made farther north. The barrage would commence one hundred and fifty yards in front of our lines. After two minutes it would creep forward at the rate of thirty yards per minute until the line of the distant Moon Trench was reached. It would continue on this line for twenty minutes and then die down.

The Colonel's orders went on : " This is in conjunction with operations by the 5th Army on the left. I have carefully checked the utmost eastern limits of our advanced posts and informed the artillery. Even allowing for progress to-night there is a margin of one hundred and fifty yards." In retaliation, the enemy might " barrage the valley about Dewdrop and Winter Trenches, and accordingly the G.O.C. wishes every available man put into Autumn and other trenches and posts in front." This meant that C and D Companies were to move up into the front line system as from 5 a.m. until such time as the commotion caused by our bluff had subsided. Details followed as to arrangements for keeping up observation during the barrage and reporting any movement, and instructions that Lewis guns should be held ready as far forward as possible so as immediately to engage any enemy seen. The real motive for moving the support companies was probably based on a fairly reasonable suspicion that the enemy gunners had got Dewdrop Trench " registered " to a nicety, but we read into it a further, if implied, compliment to the efficiency of the trenches we had dug, and rejoiced accordingly.

The night wore on as quietly as it had begun. Not a shell disturbed the double company front though the usual steady stream slid or whizzed, according to their calibre, over us to come to earth somewhere on that featureless desert behind us. About midnight Robinson reappeared, looking like some vendor of cheap jewellery at a fair. He was garlanded with watch-chains, and his pockets and haversack bulged with the haul of his gruesome search. He reported his return to me and added, " You know that shell-hole with two dead Jerries in it where I had to shelter last night, sir ? Well, there aren't two. It's the same Jerry, sir, only his head has been blown across the other side of the hole ! "

This news he gave me with the cheerful air of one correcting a piece of false information, with no hint of either horror or disgust.

Forthwith he proceeded to spread out his trophies on the fire-step as if arranging a shop-counter, and hissed like a groom does when curry-combing a horse—for many of the exhibits belonged to owners long deceased—as he made an inventory of them. There were six or seven German watches complete with chains, two gold rings, an automatic pistol, several pocket-books, which were found to contain nothing more valuable than letters and some vulgar comic post-cards, two tins of " rindfleisch " (" the poor b——'s iron rations," commented Robinson), and a pair of gloves. As he sorted them out, he kept up a running commentary in the curious barrack slang he had picked up in Malta. I interrupted him to know what he had done about the English dead, whereupon he produced from his haversack about twenty pay-books, and other articles. He made to hand these over, but I bluntly reminded him that it was his affair entirely, and that he would have to take these out with him and hand them to the Quartermaster himself. I added, " And I think it would be only decent of you to write to the relatives yourself."

The sequel has a moral. Robinson did write to several wives and mothers only to get letters back asking, for example, if he could please forward our Jim's watch, or " what became of the money my Albert had on him when he was killed." I can swear that Robinson took nothing from those bodies except the pay-books, etc., which were the price he paid for his evening's " scrounge." My aim in making him do this was to establish the identity of the nameless corpses, many of whom would certainly be reported " missing." It was a dirty and dangerous task to set a man to do—C and D Companies had on both nights sent out burying parties which had accomplished little, since the men on them had been too sick to dig !—and as it proved, a thankless one. The requests from relatives received by Robinson showed clearly how little idea they had of the circumstances in which the identity of their lost loved ones was established—hurriedly, and under shell-fire, by a corporal grubbing about in the darkness for souvenirs.

To resume. I left " Buggy Robby " parcelling out the less desirable items of his collection to members of his platoon, and got up to the front line to find Mac had just crawled in. He was hotly and fluently indignant with our guns, which he complained were firing very short. He had had a bad time out in front, and for a few tense minutes he and the sergeant had lain flattened to earth while whizz-

bangs made a " Brock's benefit " all around them.
" Just when I thought our number was up," Mac
added, " Sergeant Priestley leant towards me and in
a hoarse whisper said, ' Tell yer what, sir ; the
blokes that's firing them guns must be conscientious
objectors firing their recruit's course ' ! "—and,
disgruntled though he was, he had to laugh at what,
considering the circumstances, surely deserves a
mention in the classic dictionary of soldiers'
humour.

Mac was so insistent that it was our guns which
were firing short that I promised to report it to
Battalion Headquarters. The P.B.I. had suffered
heavily during recent weeks from their own artillery,
which was why we were prepared to damn the
gunners without reflecting upon the difficulty of
their task. The raggedness of the front line and
the absence of aiming marks must have made
accurate shooting difficult enough without the
additional handicap of mass-produced ammunition,
some of it of U.S. manufacture. It is a wonder
really that the guns were able to put down their protective or offensive barrages so close to infantry of
whose exact whereabouts there were often only hazy
notions, and yet so effectively. I must confess that
on the present occasion I stumped off down to my
Headquarters and sent off a special runner to
Battalion making charges against the artillery,
which I believe on reflection to be ill-founded. For
this reason—the salient between Lesbœufs and
Sailly Saillisel was so narrow that it is almost certain
that enemy gunners must have seized the oppor
tunity to rake our positions with enfilade fire. And
it was at the best of times practically impossible for

the unhappy recipients of such missiles to tell the exact direction from which they arrived.

The small hours of the morning passed un-eventfully. It was too cold to keep still for long, so I spent the time in moving about the line, talking to a man on sentry here, sitting down for a few minutes' smoke and yarn with a group of men there ; then taking a turn at digging to keep my circulation going. In short, the usual, tedious routine of an officer's night-life in the line—talking, shifting from one leg to another, smoking cigarette after cigarette, roaming about aimlessly or with the vague general idea of keeping the men cheerful and at work ; all the while trying to stave off sleep until " stand-to " should give at least a temporary point to existence.

I was back amongst No. 7 platoon some time before 5 p.m. so as to be ready to meet my guests from Dewdrop Trench. " Buggy " suggested to me that we might want some refreshment when they arrived, and " One or two parcels came up in rations, sir, for men who were casualties in the last show. We can't send these back, can we, sir, and there might be some good stuff in them."

To interpolate here, the usual practice was to send back again all parcels for men who had become casualties. It was a form of honesty which it is hard to believe was appreciated by the senders, who had returned to them the battered parcels they had sent to loved ones since reported killed or missing ; nor one which was carried out by any army but our own. Here the circumstances were exceptional. Carry-ing up the mail had put additional loads on ration parties already overburdened with necessities of life.

We could not carry out the parcels.   Besides, we
were short of food.   So I consented to them being
opened.   In less time than it takes to write, Robinson had been through them, and chuckled as he
brought out a tin of *café au lait* and one ditto of
cocoa *au lait*.

There came a prodigious shuffling and clanking
from away in rear, and the shapes of men loomed up
behind our trench.   Our whispered challenge was
answered by a hoarse, " D Company ! " followed
by the grumble, " Where the 'ell's A Company ? "
" Farther up the trench, mate," came from Purkiss.
" But don't make such a perishing row.   D'yer
want to *ask* Jerry to throw over a few iron rations ? "
—the only answer to which rebuke was a " Move
on, D Company," and the line of shapes shambled
off.   Their departure was followed by the equally
noisy arrival of C Company—it was impossible for
trench-accoutred men to move silently—which
drew more wrath from the occupiers, already in-
censed at being crowded out of the comparative
comfort they had contrived for themselves with so
much labour.   Naturally the newcomers were not
going to sit waist-deep in mud, so the few clean
stretches of trench were inconveniently congested.

There was much pushing and scuffling in the
darkness before the two support companies were
distributed evenly along the support trench to the
satisfaction of Hawley and Sankey, who then came
and planted themselves, their Company Sergeant-
Majors, and runners, on me.   Our fears lest they
should have been heard by the Boche proved
groundless.   Not an additional shell came over, and

cramped though we all were, we settled down as comfortably as we might to await the entertainment in which we were to be the audience if not the spectators.

Robinson was in high fettle, and promptly got his patent oven going. I can see him now standing up in the trench while we squatted or sprawled round in the darkness, his lean face lit by the faint flickering of the whale-oil lamp on which mug by mug he brewed us hot drink, talking to himself the while in his curious mixed slang, " Tray bonn, ma peach ! Now the ' doo lay ! ' Where's the panee ! Bonn for the troops ! This and a little drop of ' Tom Thumb ' will go down grand."

And he was right. Those tins of *café au lait* eked out with chlorinated water and a generous addition of rum made all of us round him, men as well as officers, the most comforting refreshment we had had for three days. It was a slow business, as only one mug could be heated at a time, but Hawley had started sipping his second ration from an almost red-hot enamel mug when suddenly the flashing of a distant line of light lit up the night sky above the trench. Silence. A great cool rush of steel overhead. Then the roar of a thousand guns rushed upon us and over us, submerging us in a sea of sound. Hawley jumped, spilt scalding liquid down his chin, swore vigorously. I yelled, " Keep down, everybody."

The command was needless. For the moment all sensations were drowned in the din of the barrage. Instinctively every one crouched a little closer to earth, though the fitful red glow of cigarettes showed that each of us was smoking feverishly, until our

nerves and ears had attuned themselves to the racket
into which we had been plunged.

Most miraculously the enemy did not retaliate—
a few extra shells " crumped " heavily into the valley
behind, but that was all, and within a few seconds
Robinson had resumed his ministrations. We
waited no longer on his cooking to circulate the
rum. We all had another tot, possibly two.
Some one started to sing " If you were the only girl
in the world." At once every one joined in.
Shades of Violet Loraine and the immortal Robey !
What matter how much noise we made ? The
enemy's ears would be ringing with our shell-
bursts, so there we sat under our moving canopy of
missiles and for nearly half an hour bawled at the
top of our voices all the favourite songs—the only
interruption a message from Mac to say that all was
well in the front line.

Then, though the cannonade still rumbled angrily
up north, the racket around us died down. We
could distinguish again the sound of individual guns,
the " double-tap " of a Hun 5.9 in. or the " Whizz-
Bang ! " of our eighteen-pounders. Except for an
occasional shot, the firing ceased. Quiet again.
We looked about us. It was dawn. Our little
interlude was over. Cramped with sitting, we rose
and stretched ourselves ; looked about us ; saw
ourselves for what we were, a set of bleary-eyed,
unshaven scallywags. Hawley said, " Well, I
don't know about you, Sankey, but I think I shall
trek back to breakfast."

And that is how we were unwittingly stall-
holders for one of the biggest shows of the Year of
Grace, 1916. A few miles north of us the 5th

Army had attacked on a wide front.   It is known to
history as the Battle of Beaumont Hamel.   But this
we only learnt afterwards.   At the time the assault
was delivered we drank, smoked, and sang with
never a thought for the thousands of lives being
choked out by bullet, bayonet, or bomb within a
few miles of us.   We were content to know some
one else was " for it."

Wearily C and D Companies dragged themselves
out and tramped back to Dewdrop Trench.   Their
departure increased the reaction from the exhilara-
tion of those fleeting minutes when we had forgotten
the present.   Now it was only the harder to get
down again to the old routine.   Memories of the
" Byng Boys," the Alhambra, the " Boche " Court
Hotel or any other association of our last leave
awakened by our singing were rudely shattered by
the sight of mud-caked wet equipment, dirty, unshaven faces, and eyes red-rimmed from want of
sleep.   Bah !   Where was the cosiness of that
trench now ?   It was nothing but a dirty ditch.

With a curt instruction to young Briggs to have
something ready for me to eat on my return, I set off
once more for the front line.   Around me the mist
eddied and swirled.

This daily round was becoming wearisome.   How
many times even during our short tour of duty of
three full days and nights had I not toiled up and
down the same earthen alleyway, to and from
similar alleyways ?   Had I been older, more
maturely reflective, I might have asked myself what
was the point of it all.   Even as it was, some words
came back to me that my college tutor had written
in his last letter home before dying by a sniper's

bullet in front of Ypres. " This is a boring show," he had written, " more stupid even than dangerous." At this distance I think he described the war in one phrase better than all the peeps into hell purveyed by a best-selling war novelist to a credulous public.

But at the time I only knew that things were getting depressingly and tiringly monotonous. After all, most of us were too young to have any standards of comparison. This was our life. We had been pitchforked headlong into khaki from school or college. The war was just another experience as first our preparatory school, and then our public school had been. We were not philosophers in uniform. The majority of us were hardly mature enough to philosophise at all.

There was no doubt about the mist that morning. It was reported as a " fog " in the divisional intelligence reports. It was just such a morning as in England would disorganise suburban train services and cause City men to arrive at their offices late and angry. And on such a morning at Cambridge, I reflected, I should have pulled the blankets a little closer round my ears and called to my " bedder " to stand the hot water can in front of the fire to warm for a bath. I should certainly have " cut " my early lecture. Even at the moment, my father would probably be coughing at the rawness of the morning as he set out to take early service in the village church. All over the world, in city or in hamlet, folk would be going about their business, while I ploughed through mud and mist in an endeavour to keep happy and efficient a hundred and fifty men living an existence as monotonous as my own.

But whatever it might have done at home, to us the fog came as a blessing. It lay like a fleecy blanket across the front, enforcing inactivity on both sides by robbing war of its eyes. Not a shot was being fired from gun or rifle, and as I entered the front line, there was no sound except the coughing or subdued voices of weary men to break the stillness. One or two more energetic than the rest stamped up and down, clapping their sides to keep the circulation going. The machine-gun still pointed steadfastly at Cemetery Circle, though now it was covered with a ground-sheet. There was nothing to be done.

When I met Mac he told me that he had had an experience even more novel than ours. It appeared that, simultaneously with the 5th Army's offensive far away to the left, the French had attacked on a smaller scale some few hundred yards to our right, and the front line troops had found themselves in the orchestra stalls for a battle-piece. According to Mac the spectacle was so fantastic as to be scarcely credible. Pressing the metaphor of the theatre, the stage, seen through the curtain of the early morning mist, was lit by the dancing flames of the barrage, the din of which, drowning all else, gave the scene the muted movement of a silent film. According to Mac's description, he found himself sitting on the fringe of a downpour of shells confined to his satisfaction and comfort neatly in an area far enough away for his men to be quite out of danger. On this stage the earth leapt and spouted like a river lashed by giant hailstones. The "heavies" threw up slow geysers of flying earth to the accompaniment of rolling thunder. The sharp crackle of shrapnel, daubing the smoky grey with splashes of angry red, blended with the swift, bustling clatter of the 75's: followed swiftly by the harsh patter of the machine-guns in concealed chorus and the final breathless popping of musketry as the French left their trenches, advancing in ragged lines to the assault. Mac explained how now and again they disappeared into the rolling banks of smoke, emerged, halted until their barrage strode on, advanced again—then suddenly the leading wave of blue-grey figures rushed into the forward German positions. From our trench the men could see helmeted Germans rising incredibly out of the powdered earth, see them fire, turn to run, surrender, or lug their heavy machine-guns out of action. On went the scene, a slowly moving torrent of flying earth and steel, until it flowed over the ridge and passed out of sight, the pale gleams of winter daylight slowly dispersing the mist and revealing a now empty stage where a battle, seen as in a dream, had been fought out a few minutes before.

So that last day in the line passed under its mantle of fog. The short winter daylight passed in uneasy silence. The men slept ; took their turn at a meaningless spell of duty at the sentry-posts, peering stupidly into the mist; and wrote letters or " Whizz-Bangs " to be posted home when we got out—" I am well," " I am in hospital," etc. " Cross out the words which do not apply."

Robbed of their eyes in the air, even the heavy guns were still, but one of the few shells which our field guns fired, burst short in the very mouth of A Company's sap, killing two men.

The piece of news sent me off post haste to Fall Trench to investigate. Cropper was in the sap

when I arrived. The shell that had done the
damage had come from directly in rear, otherwise it
could not have entered the trench as it had done.
It had burst plumb in the middle of the sap-way,
killing the two men instantaneously but without
mutilating them much. There was little room for
doubt that it was one of our own shells, and that was
removed when, after a few seconds poking about in
the smoke-blackened soil, we found the nosecap.
It was a British eighteen-pounder. It was only
natural to curse the gunners, the rotten American
ammunition, the worn guns, the inefficiency of the
intelligence people who did not know where their
own bloody infantry were, the staff, and every one
else whom we could think of for blotting out two
good Yorkshire soldiers. But, living as we were in
scoops and burrows which not only were not shown
on any map, but which we ourselves were frantically
anxious should be difficult to detect by direct
observation, we were as much at the mercy of our
own as of the enemy gunners. And when we had
blown off our indignation, we had to admit that the
marvel was that such accidents did not happen more
often. Anyway, there was nothing to be done. I
promised Cropper I would report to Battalion Headquarters so that they could pass the information
on to our divisional artillery. Cropper undertook
to see that the victims were buried as soon as night
fell, so that we might leave everything shipshape for
the Worcesters.

From A Company's sap to that of B Company
was only a few yards along Fall Trench, and my visit
took the post there, consisting of a young lance-
corporal and two men, by surprise. The corporal

had not only allowed his men to take off their equipment, but was minus his own, while there was a
general atmosphere of slackness. It was strictly
against orders to remove any essential equipment
while in the trenches, and the offence naturally
became still more heinous in men on what was
virtually outpost duty. Still, in view of the youth
of the N.C.O. and his good record, I was prepared to
let him off this time with a good dressing-down, had
he not shown a kind of familiar resentment that I
should have taken exception to his indiscipline.
This hint of familiarity touched me on a delicate
spot. It had always seemed absurd to me to try and
adhere rigidly to the conventional formalities of
discipline in the trenches where officers lived cheek
by jowl with their men, shared the same dangers, the
same dug-outs, and sometimes the same mess-tins.
Quite apart from the absurdity, I believed, and
nothing I ever saw subsequently shook me in the
belief, that the way to get the best out of the British
soldier was for an officer to show that he was the
friend of his men, and to treat them as friends.
This naturally involved a relaxation of pre-war codes
of behaviour, but it did not mean that an officer
should rub shoulders with his men at every opportunity, or allow them to become familiar with him.
It meant rather that he should step down from the
pedestal on which his rank put him, and walk easily
among his men, relying on his own personality and
the respect he had earned from them to give him the
superior position he must occupy if he wished to
lead. He had consequently to steer a delicate
course between treating those under him as equals in
humanity if inferiors in status, and losing their

respect by becoming too much one of them.   He must deal with them sympathetically and at all times interpret the law in the spirit and not in the letter, but he had equally to be jealous of his position, and never to allow leniency to be looked upon as weakness, or friendship to degenerate into familiarity. He had, in short, to discriminate between the men who would appreciate his interest and those who would be foolish enough to try and impose upon his good-nature.

This was a case in point.   Nothing was left to me but to take disciplinary action, and sending for his platoon commander, Hall, I ordered him to be relieved of his post and brought up for punishment when we got out of the line.   For that show of bad manners, he was to lose his lance-stripe.

It was but a few moments before our minds were turned to less serious thoughts.   Hall and I had walked a little farther along to the right of the sector —we were standing talking in the front line when we noticed a scuffling of earth in the parados of the trench, and out fell a furry, fat little mole.   It appeared as one of Nature's miracles that this blind, slow creature could have survived in ground so pounded and upturned.   After holding him for a few minutes, and marvelling at the strength of his tiny limbs, we put him into his hole again to find his way back whence he had come.   A few desperate clawings, and he had disappeared.   How we wished we could dig ourselves in so easily !

As darkness drew on, the mist lifted, and Purkiss, as company cook, and the officers' servants were sent out of the line to make ready the camp against our arrival.   They were a reluctant party that set off over the top, loath to leave the comparative safety of their forward position to cross that dreaded two miles of shell-swept mud separating us from the nearest approach to civilised comforts.

Darkness took the place of fog, but the effect was much the same. The day had been but a continuation of the night. The only difference was that night was the time of movement. Just as an English countryside comes to life after dark, when even the roadside hedge is quick with rustlings and squeakings, so the dead landscape of the Somme stirred into activity with nightfall. And as we listened to the now familiar far-off rumble of transport behind the enemy lines as behind our own, there was this evening the knowledge that soon we were to be relieved, to go back out of this outpost to some camp where we should have braziers and blankets and hot food. We had all been through it before, most of us more times than we could remember. We were familiar with every dreary detail of relief as we were of taking-over, yet there was no one of us, not even the most hardened campaigner, who would not confess to being seized on every such occasion with the fear that at the last moment something dreadful would happen, some disaster overtake him before he had passed through the danger zone which separated the line from the safety of the back areas. It might come by a chance sniper's bullet, striking him down noiselessly before he even got out of the trenches. It might come with a scream out of the darkness when the worst of the journey lay behind him.

So it was on this night of November 13. The marvel of three days without rain had enabled us more quickly than usual to get the trenches clean and tidy, to collect our kit, and put ourselves in readiness to depart as soon as the Worcesters should appear. The result was that the men were waiting for the relief almost as soon as night fell, and tried to keep their spirits up, after the manner of the British soldier, by singing all the most mournful ditties they knew from " Don't go down the Mine, Daddy," to " Oh My, I don't want to Die ! I want to go Home."

I had to make a final last trip round the sector, noting with a certain pride the improvements that the kindness of the elements had allowed us to make. Not only had we temporarily subjugated the mud, but we had added another brand-new piece to the great jig-saw puzzle of the trench system of the Western Front. There were also arrangements to be made with Mac about moving the company out. We had been ordered to salvage as much derelict equipment and stores as possible, and that meant putting further burdens in the shape of waterproof capes, sheets, or great-coats on to already tired and overladen men. But there was another point, and one which served to show me how very easy it is to write orders which were capable of more than one interpretation. I, for some incomprehensible reason, had read the command about Company Commanders reporting "relief complete " at Battalion Head-quarters, to mean that I, at the head of my straggling followers, was to flounder through the mud to that death-trap the Sunken Road, and, while they awaited almost certain destruction, inform the Adjutant that we had handed over properly and without incident. I waxed righteously indignant. Whatever was the

Colonel thinking about, I asked Mac, giving orders so unlike him in their disregard of the men's safety ! Anyway, I would do nothing of the sort. If I had to report personally I would report alone, and Mac should take the company out by the quickest and easiest way he could find. I would meet him at Ginchy cross-roads.

One, two, nearly three hours dragged by with the men getting more restive and anxious to be gone. The enemy left us alone, confining his " frightful-ness " to the valley behind. This was a temporary blessing only, causing each one of us to shrink the more from the thought of the journey we should have to make. We had become such troglodytes that to leave the shelter of a trench induced a feeling of nakedness. Not until nearly eleven o'clock did there come the welcome sounds of men approaching, and the Worcesters began filing in. They had had a rotten time in the passage of the valley, poor devils, much worse than we had had, and had lost several men. Still, favoured by the weather and undis-turbed by " Fritz," the ceremony of handing-over was accomplished with all possible haste and, shep-herded by the lanky Mac, the company struggled out on their journey to Ginchy. Unlike the Devons, we left no rum behind us !

As soon as the last man was clear of the trenches, I started out for Battalion Headquarters in the Sunken Road, so confident in my ability to find it that I took no orderly with me. Alas for such pre-sumption ! I had gone no more than a few dozen paces when I began to have misgivings. Surely, I should have passed Dewdrop Trench by now. I paused to take what bearings I could, but the night

was black as pitch. Landmarks there were none.
A shell burst here and there, and I remember thinking what a wrong impression the ordinary war
pictures gave. They always showed shells exploding with a vivid flash, but all that now happened was
a scream, a thud, and a little shower of red sparks as
from a blacksmith's anvil. There was not the
faintest glimmer to light me on my way. I stumbled
on. Doubts became anxiety. I was lost ! No
matter that I ought to know I could not be far away
from some one ; I was afraid. Throughout the
war this was my worst nightmare—to be alone, and
lost and in danger. Worse than all the anticipation
of battle, all the fear of mine, raid, or capture, was
this dread of being struck down somewhere where
there was no one to find me, and where I should lie
till I rotted back slowly into the mud. I had seen
those to whom it had happened.

So now anxiety passed almost at once into panic.
I went forward more quickly first at a sharper walk,
then at a desperate blundering trot. Was it
imagination ? Or were more shells really beginning
to fall, rushing down to sink into the soft earth
and burst with smothered thuds ? Yes ! Little
showers of red sparks were all around me. I
struggled on, fell once, again, many times, tore my
coat on barbed wire, cut my hand. When would a
bullet from those chattering machine-guns strike me
in the head or back ? The nape of my neck ran
cold at the thought. My heart thumped louder
than ever, both from terror and effort. I was getting
blown. I could go no further. Then I stumbled,
pitched forward, slithered down several 'feet,
caught my kit on some signal wires, sank up to

my elbows in wet mud. I had reached the Sunken Road !

Breathless and shaken, I struggled to my feet. A head peered at me out of a sand-bagged dug-out entrance. I asked the owner the whereabouts of the West Yorkshire headquarters. He thought there were some infantry battalion headquarters a little farther up the road on the opposite side, but whose he did not know. He was a signaller, he confessed, as if to excuse his lack of information. There was nothing for it but to find out for myself.

What a cess-pit that Sunken Road was ! Over ankle-deep in slime, it was strewn with the bodies of horses and mules in varying stages of decay. Yet its battered banks afforded the only convenient cover for a wide area around, so into them had been driven dug-outs, British and German, into which were crammed all those whose duties kept them in the forward zone without taking them into the trenches. There were the headquarters of two or three battalions, the forward posts of batteries, both field and heavy, signallers, sappers, and odd details of all arms. I made shouted inquiries down two or three shafts before I pulled aside the tattered sandbag cover which hung before the right dug-out, and entered a tiny candle-lit burrow. In it were installed the Worcesters. My own regiment had gone!

This was the crowning blow. With apologies for my intrusion, I set out again into the darkness, feeling more wretched and hopeless than ever after the brief vision of light and warmth. But this time luck was with me, and hardly had I scrambled up the bank than some one said, " Who's there ? " and I recognised Hawley's voice. He was making for

Ginchy with an orderly who knew the way, so we set
off together.   With company the whole atmosphere
seemed to change.   The danger remained the
same, yet the presence of others banished at once the
terror that had assailed me.   In a few minutes we
were passing battery positions and were dazzled by
the stabbing, lemon flashes of the guns as they fired
towards us.   Then we struck the duck-board track
which, rickety and shell-smashed though it was,
lead us steadily towards Ginchy.   Lights again
began to appear in dug-out doors and gun-positions,
now far enough away from the enemy to disregard
the risk of detection, and at last we were able to make
out groups of men in the darkness.   We had made
Ginchy cross-roads, and the men were B Company
in artillery formation, into which Mac had put them
to lessen the danger from any chance shell.   Thanks
to his guidance in avoiding the bad places, they had
got out without loss.

Without wasting time in marvelling at this
miracle, the Company fell in and moved off.   That
march was a nightmare.   Not till then did I realise
how tired I was, nor how done the men.   I had
snatched less sleep than they—my total for the three
days was no more than six hours—and had been
more continuously " on the go."   They, on the
other hand, were overloaded with sodden kit.   We
had not gone far before requests were made for a
halt.   I turned a deaf ear.   Men so weary, I
argued, would only fall asleep the moment they
broke rank.   It would be the harder to get them on
the move again.   Besides, we were still in the shelled
area.   Requests turned to protests.   Some of the
younger men could hardly walk.   Officers and the

fresher N.C.O.s took over rifles and packs from the most fatigued but without avail. The querulous, half-mutinous demands for rest grew more insistent. They were the cries of semiconscious minds tortured by over-exertion and lack of sleep. Still I took no notice, vowing that not until we were in the haven of our own camp would I call a halt. " I won't stop ! I won't stop ! I won't stop ! " I repeated to myself with each agonising step. My ears, deaf to all else, sung the refrain. But to no purpose. Will said, " I won't stop " ; Body argued, " I can't go on." And so it was. After what seemed hours of tramping I could go no farther. All my determination was thrown to the winds. " Halt ! " I could do no more than speak the command. It was enough. The word was scarce uttered before every one, myself included, had thrown himself down on to the bricks and rubbish at the roadside. There we lay, silent, exhausted. Will began to reassert itself. This was no good. The longer we stayed the more difficult it would be to go on. Somehow, how I do not know, we stirred and prodded the men into movement again. Cursing and grunting, they shambled forward with the unsteady steps of sleepwalkers. I tried to square my shoulders for the long march that I felt must lie ahead. Irony of ironies ! We had not moved more than a few score paces before the gruff voice of Company Sergeant-Major Scott was heard shouting " This way, B Company." We had fallen out less than a hundred yards from camp !

But what miles we must have marched ! How many was it ? The distance from Ginchy cross-roads to La Briqueterie camp was no more than three and a half miles ! The front line was under five miles away. There is no doubt the Somme taught us that distance is a relative term, not to be measured in yards and feet.

Once again we were under canvas, La Briqueterie being a camp of bell-tents where once had stood the brickyard which had figured so prominently in the dispatches describing the September battles around Montauban. Unlike the pitiful " Camp 34 " at Trones Wood, La Briqueterie would not have been entirely disgraced by comparison with the real thing as seen at Aldershot or on Salisbury Plain. Tents were pitched in regular lines, and were well and truly guyed with a brazier alight and glowing in each one, and dear old Hinchcliffe, the Quartermaster, ready to issue hot soup and rum for every man. We felt we had fallen into luxury indeed. Lord ! How the keen edge of appreciation of creature comforts is blunted by a life of peace ! Did not a mess-tin of stew, a tot of rum or whisky and water in a tin mug, taste more like divine nectar than the best champagne drunk out of the finest cut-glass to-day ? To enjoy ease, it is surely necessary to labour. To enjoy luxury, it is necessary to live hard. Since our work in these after-days is all too often sedentary, since we all too often tend to overfeed, and since we shun living hard, if we have not lost the capacity for it, it is small wonder that we are dyspeptically out of tune with life, and have to pay to have our jaded appetites whetted by manufactured thrills on stage, screen, dirt-track, or playing field. No such necessity existed in France in the war years. The enemy provided excitement enough.

However it may be, our spirits rose and our mouths watered at the delectable prospect which had opened so suddenly out of the night. Mac and George I sent to take off their equipment, staying myself to watch Company Quartermaster-Sergeant Carlton allot tents to the company, and Company Sergeant-Major Scott start to serve out the soup. Having seen things properly started, I went off to remove my burdensome equipment before returning to supervise the rum issue. As my guide led me to the officers' lines, he pointed to a great hole which yawned where the next tent to ours had stood. " That was your tent this afternoon, sir," he told me, " but about two hours ago Jerry dropped an eight-inch shell there and ' napoo-ed ' it." He reassured me that this had been the only shell the enemy had put into the camp. Still, that hole would have been a disquieting feature in a rest camp had it not been that I was too tired to do more than register its presence as a fact.

I had barely started to take off my kit when an orderly came to say, " Colonel wants you in B Company lines at once, sir." Tearing off the bulkiest items of my " Christmas Tree," I hurried back to find the Colonel standing with Scott.

"What does this mean?" he demanded. "Don't you know yet that an officer's place is with his men? Haven't you learnt yet that an officer has no right to think of his own comfort until he has satisfied himself that every one of his men is comfortable? Not only that, but you go away to your tent and leave a warrant officer to issue rum, which is entirely against all orders." I struggled to explain that my offence was not so heinous as it seemed. I had not left until the men had been settled in and soup was being issued. I had had no intention of staying away, and I had given no instructions to any one to issue rum. At this the Colonel calmed down, and I recount the incident to illustrate his determination that the welfare of his men should be the first concern of every officer. I accompanied him through the lines, and that he was satisfied was soon evident as he left me with an invitation to come round to Battalion Headquarters for a drink when I had finished.

Although this was evidence of forgiveness, I rounded on Scott, asking why in Heaven he, of all people, had presumed to issue rum. His answer that he had done so quite deliberately because he had thought I had had about enough, and it was one way in which he could help me, completely disarmed me, and the stinging rebuke which I had contemplated turned to thanks.

At long last our duties were at an end. Every man was bedded down in warmth and with a belly reasonably full of soup and rum. It was nearly two o'clock. Bidding Scott good-night I turned thankfully towards the tent allotted to the Headquarters Mess. This I found brightly lit and almost inconveniently crowded. The Colonel was there, and Maclaren, and Matheson, and young Rayner, the assistant Adjutant, who like poor Skett was a recent arrival from Sandhurst and like him too, destined not to survive the war. There were cheery greetings, and Brownlow, imperturbable as ever, brought a whisky and soda. As I drank it the Colonel congratulated me on the behaviour of A and B Companies during the tour, and apologised for his testiness in " strafing " me. He too was overtired.

His appreciation, coupled with a second whisky and soda, gave me a pleasurably warm feeling. Life took on a different complexion. Everything was good. Every one was friendly. I stayed chatting with Matheson for a few minutes, long enough to learn that the Boche had in fact put down a barrage as we were coming out—so that shelling when I lost my way was not imagination, I registered to myself —and D Company had been caught in it, though providentially without losing a man. Since we had last met two of our friends had gone West, but except for a passing reference—" rotten luck "— their names were not mentioned. We were glad to be out, to be alive, and be together again.

I said my good-nights and sallied forth into the night air. Could I walk to my tent ? Could I even stand ? No ! Two whiskies and soda on an empty stomach and in my exhausted physical condition had made me so drunk that I had to crawl home on all fours. Too tired and too fuddled to undress, I struggled out of jacket and boots, rolled into my flea-bag, and almost before I lay down had joined my snores to those of Mac and George.

V

THE WAY BACK

V

THE WAY BACK

By the Colonel's dispensation, we rose at a very unregimental hour next morning, and it was after 9 a.m. when Briggs undid the tent-flap and brought in a mug of hot water for shaving. Here was luxury indeed! Not for five days had I washed, shaved, or looked at myself in a glass. Now when, still too drowsily comfortable to get up, I sat up in my flea-bag and saw what I looked like, I burst out laughing. " Bearded like the pard " does an injustice to that noble animal. The beard which covered my face could better be likened to some charred gorse-bush. And Mac said as much. What joy it was to lather and feel the razor shearing off this unwelcome growth ! How different, how much fresher I felt when the somewhat painful operation was complete. Then and not till then, I got up, stretched, put my head in the canvas bucket of water outside the tent, and washed. The transformation was magical. Spiritually and in appearance I was a different being. Youth has a surprising resilience, and memories of the dirt, discomforts, and dangers of the past four days were sloughed off with the soap and water and the application of a razor.

We were ready for breakfast, a real breakfast once more, with bacon and fried bread and hot tea. This we devoured seated on our flea-bags, interrupted

only by a Headquarters' runner to say that the
Colonel was holding orderly room at 11 a.m.

We were so late in finishing breakfast that we
were forced to scramble down to the Company lines
in some haste to satisfy ourselves that there were no
defaulters, before I had to repair to Battalion Orderly
Room.   Here were many cheery reunions as
officers and warrant officers assembled, especially
with Palmes and others who had been left out of the
line.   Pym's disappearance was the topic of the
hour.   The fact that he was only a few yards from
Fall Trench when he had vanished ; the fact that he
had ordered his men back when the enemy machine-
gun had opened fire, suggesting that he had not
himself been hit ;   the fact that he had never
answered our calls to him nor had any trace of him
been found—these were agreed by all to present a
mysterious picture.   What had happened to him ?
We were busy with conjecture when the Colonel
arrived with the Brigadier, who announced himself
as very pleased with the work the Battalion had done
while in the front line.   He also complimented the
Colonel on the smoothness and rapidity with which
the relief had been carried out, and so far away
already was the memory of that age-long march of a
few hours previously that no one saw anything in his
remark to smile at.   We were all standing round
him, I right in front of him, when he turned to ask
the Colonel where I was.   Amid general laughter
it transpired that having only seen me in my unshorn
and mud-plastered state he did not recognise me.
It was a long time before I heard the last of that !

Following the G.O.C.'s departure, the routine
duties of Battalion office were soon over, and we

dismissed to our respective commands to bear the glad news that the day would be spent in cleaning up, that there would therefore be no parades other than the necessary fatigues, and that on the morrow we were to move back again to the Citadel whence we had set out a week before. " Cleaning-up " was in itself no mean task, involving as it did, not only the scraping and brushing of kits and boots, the cleaning of rifles and bayonets and the polishing of buttons, but the more intimate details of " de-lousing," or as the Yorkshiremen termed it, " chat-ting " themselves. In every tent I visited, one or more men were to be seen sitting naked to the waist exploring the seams of their shirts with a lighted candle to destroy the " chats " which had bred and mustered during the past four days. This opera-tion was a never-failing source of crude humour. " I'm making a collection, Nobby," I heard one man say, " I've got all kinds now except one with pink eyes and revolving teeth," and " Have you got any swaps, Nigger ? "

On my way back to my tent I met the Doctor, who had only been posted to the Battalion ten days previously, his predecessor having been killed during our last tour in the line.

" I suppose you had a ' cushy ' time of it, Doctor," I said. " Two officers and sixteen ranks isn't a very big bag for four days, is it ? "

" No," he replied, with a grim smile, " but you forget that this is a war of attrition. It's not only the enemy that causes the casualties. Why, I had more men at sick parade this morning than we lost in the line ! And I had to evacuate four of them. I can do nothing for any one who is really sick."

" Is there much sickness ? " I asked.

" There are a good many cases of p.u.o. and nephritis at the moment.   Oh, if you want to know what those are, p.u.o. means ' pyrrhexia of unknown origin,' commonly known as trench fever ;   and nephritis is a form of kidney trouble caused by all this wet and cold.   But what amazes me is that there is practically no malingering and comparatively little serious illness.   Still, I should like to see a comparison made between the losses per battalion on the Somme now from enemy action and from the wastage caused by minor ailments, such as frostbite, trench-feet, and other causes.   I think it would be illuminating."   He nodded and moved off.

A lugubrious person the new Doctor, I thought, but two of his observations set me thinking.   First, it *was* extraordinary that a trivial complaint which in the easy days of peace would have been sufficient to warrant medical attention, medicine, or a day away from work, was not nowadays deemed to justify the sufferer reporting sick, possibly because he knew that he had to be ill indeed before he got his ticket of escape from " the Somme."   Secondly, and even more astonishing, was the policy of the British Army regarding regimental doctors.   At a time when all the medical skill the world could mobilise was so desperately wanted, we alone of the nations engaged were content to waste so many qualified men by maintaining a medical officer with each battalion. As the Doctor had observed, the regimental medical officer had practically no opportunities of making use of his special knowledge.   All he could do was to ensure that the latrines were properly sited and disinfected ;   take the daily sick parade, and evacuate any one who was ill to the Field Ambulance ; and see that his orderlies and stretcher-bearers were well-drilled and capable of discharging their duties efficiently. He could, in short, accomplish little more than a trained Royal Army Medical Corps non-commissioned officer. The stock argument for his being maintained was the familiar one that a doctor was necessary for *morale*. But it was a heavy price we had to pay. Our present doctor was the third we had had in as many months, and doctors are not trained in a year.

Despite the late hour at which we had break-fasted we were more than ready for luncheon, the menu for which Parkin announced in his richest Rotherham accents as " Stewed beef and sixty-pounders, sir, and deaf'uns and coostard," which may be translated as stewed beef with suet dumplings and figs and custard ! Anyway it was, if memory serves, a very sumptuous and succulent repast, to which we did ample justice, and, afterwards, con-tentedly full, curled ourselves up for a post-prandial snooze.

From this we were awakened by the sound of music, and hastened out to find the band of one of the Guards regiments playing in an adjoining camp. This phenomenon was proving a great draw, and men were trekking from all points of the compass to witness a spectacle so unexpected albeit so welcome. There was something curious to us in the appearance of these trim, well-drilled bandsmen, so reminiscent even in their khaki of the Mall or the Horse Guards, as there was in the civilised or civilising effect of their music in this vast rubbish heap populated with human ants. It gave us each a secret glow of satisfaction to feel that such things could still be, to know that people were still being trained for other things than digging, bombing, or bayonet-fighting. We stayed till the performance ended, then turned back to our tents with a lighter step.   Music hath power as well as charms.

There was a message awaiting me from Palmes that I should go and dine with him and C Company's other officers.   That meant there was only the interval between tea and dinner to fill in, and apart from a visit to the company lines, this was accomplished with the aid of a bottle of whisky and some cigarettes, over which Mac, George, and I discussed Pym's disappearance again from all angles.   None of us could make head or tail of it.   George told us that the men were saying openly that Pym had been a German spy.   We laughed, of course.   " But," George went on, " Where did he come from ? The Canadians !   I know ! but which Canadians ? What battalion ?   Who knew him ?   Came here from an officers' school.   Yes, but couldn't any one pinch another bloke's papers and come the same way ?   And who knew him when he was with the Battalion ?   Going off every night to Beuvry, Bethune, or some other ' red-lamp ' place.   The other A Company officers never knew him.   You ask them when you go round there to-night."

I promised to do so.   Naturally the mystery was further discussed over dinner—made noteworthy by a very realistic if sooty imitation of a sweet omelette prepared by Palmes' cook—without further elucidation.   The discussion did, however, draw from Palmes a few pithy comments on discipline. " Whatever did happen to Pym," Palmes said, " the incident proves what I have always held to be true. It's not a ha'porth of good being a brave man or a gallant leader if you don't take the trouble to know your men or get them to know you while you are out at rest.   From the little I saw of him—Pym only joined us in the Hohenzollern about six weeks ago— I should say he was full of guts.   In the line he was personally brave and ready to go anywhere.   Out of the line he was quite different.   He wouldn't bother himself with the men or interest himself in them. You can see it in the way he went out finally.   Did he go along the trench and detail three or four men by name, men he knew, to follow him out to dig the sap ?   No—he stood up on the parapet in the darkness and said, ' You, and you, and you, get a spade and come out here ! '   He did not know whom he had with him.   They hardly knew him by sight.   The result was that when that machine-gun opened and he called to them to get back, they all went.   If he had been known to his men, you don't tell me one or two of them would not have stayed to see he too was coming in with them.   And the awful part of that sort of thing is that not only is Pym himself missing, but a good boy like young Skett gets killed."

This question of the relative values of discipline and gallantry was a favourite thesis of Palmes', but it did less than justice to Pym.   When he called " Retire " out of the darkness, the best men would, and should have obeyed, not doubting in the scramble that their officer was with them.   Then it was probable, we argued, that he had been mortally wounded with just enough breath left in his body to call the one word before collapsing.   Or again, he

might have been badly hit and have been seized by a
German patrol, dragged back unconscious to the
enemy lines, and died there. So we discussed the
matter at great length until the growing chilliness of
the tent warned us that it was time to turn in and try
and make up some of the sleep that we had missed
during the past four days.

But the disappearance of Pym must remain a real
mystery of the Great War.

There was no long lie-in next morning. Reveille
on the 15th was at 6 a.m. of a damp morning.
The Battalion was to move off at 9 a.m. As
we dressed, shivering and miserable, the servants
were busy packing up our kits and blankets.
Breakfast was the usual hurried, unsatisfying affair,
eaten in haste with Parkin muttering that the
" Transport officer is waiting for the baggage, sir."
Oh ! the discomfort of those winter moves—the
rolling, stacking, and loading of blankets, the packing of valises, of cooking-pots and utensils, the
haste, the sweat, the cursings, and the bad tempers !
But, as usual, out of apparent chaos the miracle of
order and punctuality was contrived, and the Battalion fell in by companies outside their tents to drag
themselves and their Lewis-gun carts across the five
and a half miles that separated La Briqueterie from the
Citadel. As soon as we were fairly on the road the
congestion was found to be worse even than that we
had experienced before. Moreover, we now had
with us those accursed Lewis-gun carts. Never were
invented such lunatic vehicles ! It was as if the
designer had deliberately set out to evolve the most
difficult item of infantry transport. Resembling a

species of shortened coffin, they were mounted on
two low wheels and provided with handles which
were so near the ground that the wretched pusher
had to bend almost double to grip them. Of
effective leverage he could have none, and even with
a human trace-horse pulling in front, the task of
moving or steering the carts on a good road was not
a light one. On the slowly moving river of transport and mud on which we found ourselves embarked
it was impossible. As a choice of evils it was
decided to detail sufficient men to take them by a
geographically short cut across country, while the
remainder of the Battalion fought their way down
the road. It is useless to attempt to describe the
efforts and sufferings of those Lewis-gun teams.

To any one not there to see for himself, it is
difficult even to give a picture of the back areas of
the Somme in that winter of 1916.

Imagine a countryside resembling, though not so
steeply hilly as, the South Downs around Alfriston
and Seaford. Strip it of every vestige of green.
Denude it of every wood, copse, or village. Pound
it with shell-fire until it is a putty-coloured wilderness, showing white scars here and there where
deeper explosions or tunnel dug-outs have penetrated
to the chalk. Litter it with all the dirt and débris of
the battlefield. Then dump on it a vast army of
men, housed in tents, hutments, bivouacs, and dug-
outs, so close to one another that the area is one
great camping-ground, scattered with horse-lines,
drinking-troughs, battery and wagon standings,
with here and there a long-range gun emplacement
or a heavy howitzer poking its snub nose skywards.
Finally, plaster the whole incredible scene with a

thick layer of mud, and you will have some picture, if but an inadequate one, of what it looked like. See the poor animals, horses and mules, standing patiently up to the hocks in slush, their coats, despite the devoted attentions of their owners, caked with mud.   The mules, be it noted, were less objects for sympathy than the horses, for the mule was a comical, self-reliant brute, and though his face was a mask of clay there was something very humorous in the way he semaphored with his long ears, and cocked them at droll angles.   The day being relatively fine, a number of observation balloons, like inflated pigs, swung on their mooring ropes in the sky. How like an overturned nest of slow termites the scene below them must have appeared to the observers.

But whether we jostled and splashed along the road or sweated and laboured with the Lewis-gun carts across country, we had neither the time nor the spirit to look about us.   That march was a repetition of our journey up the line, with the one difference, that it now forgot to rain.   Otherwise there was the same plodding in Indian file, ankle deep in mud, dodging the interminable chain of wagons, guns, ambulances, and staff cars, the same wearisome halts, the same panting starts to recover lost distance.   After some time the road improved and the traffic thinned enough to enable something approaching column of route to be formed.   At any rate the battalion managed to proceed in fours by platoons, although at large and irregular intervals. And this was as well, as all of a sudden with a steady swing a battalion of the Guards passed us, marching towards the line.   Very fine and soldierlike they looked, all big men, carrying their marching order with an enviable ease, and with their khaki new and clean. There was not a man among us who did not brace himself up and strive to look his best as they went by, determined to uphold the prestige of a line regiment in the face of these picked troops, whom we secretly looked up to, but openly envied for what we imagined to be the favoured treatment they received. Did they not have five mess-carts per battalion as against our one ? Did they not usually get the best billets ? Did they not have the pick of the men ? Why, a Guards recruit earned the recruiting sergeant 2s. 6d. instead of the humble shilling he got for a linesman. These were but some of the comments to be overheard in the ranks, together with many other grouses as to better food and more plentiful issues of clothing and stores, which were possibly unjust. Acting on the Colonel's principle that we must never let the men run down the Guards, I reminded one of the grousers that, whatever their privileges, the Guards were in every big scrap and were never known to let a show down. " Yes, sir, but they ought to do well, going in with full bellies and new kit, and having pioneers to dig their trenches for them." This last was a libel, but I recognised in it an allusion to the Guards Pioneer Battalion we had recently seen improving a camp for one of the regiments of the Guards Division. Anyway, I thought, however many suits of clothes the Guards might have, we did not cut such a bad figure by comparison with them. Granted that our men were shorter, and that we were coming out after a week in the mud, the regiment were surprisingly spick and span. The one day spent at La Briqueterie had been well-spent in

cleaning up.   Colonel Jack's diary describes the
incident in a nutshell :

" Passed Guards Battalion on way to front.   Very
clean and smart.   But 2 W. York. had got themselves marvellously straightened up in the two
days of semi-peace under bad conditions.   Very
fine fellows indeed."

Which shows that he, too, did not fear the
comparison.

At long last we came in sight of the familiar,
dirty bell-tents and the high bank, riddled with old
German dug-outs, of Citadel Camp.   Turning
thankfully off the road on to the softer mud of the
Camp, Companies were led by guides to their tents.
It was 12.30 p.m.   That five miles of marching
had occupied three and a half strenuous hours of
labour.   No wonder that we were again tired, nor
that our stomachs reminded us that we had break-
fasted early.   But once again our hopes of food were
shattered.   Before the tents were allotted or the
men had had time to take off their equipment, the
rumour fled round that the transport had not
arrived.   With the transport were the cookers, and
in the cookers were the regiment's dinners !   A
bitter blow indeed.   It was not that we were merely
angry at being cheated out of a meal.   Ravenous and
tired though we were, our disappointment was
something more than that of a diner who comes to
table to find the meal on which he had set his heart
is not ready, that the cook is out, and the provisions
have not arrived.   Figure it for yourself.   Here
were we arrived in our camp, actually in occupation
of our tents, we could take off our marching order
and ease our shouders, but could we make ourselves

at home ? Of course not. Not only were the cookers miles behind, in that jam of transport, but so were the wagons with our blankets and all the precious odds and ends that were to enable us to transform a bell-tent from a mere canvas shelter on uncompromising bare boards into the fuggy, furnished habitations in which we could with a little ingenuity and luck imagine ourselves to be comfortable. The most we could do at the moment was to moon about, waiting for the missing vehicles to turn up, momentarily becoming more conscious of wet feet and the chilliness of the November breeze. We just hung around, shivering, talking idly to one another and cursing the Somme, the roads, and everything on which we could blame this misfortune. Those lucky enough to have any, smoked cigarette after cigarette ; not only did even " Ruby Queens " or " Red Hussars "—whoever named those weird war-brands of " gaspers " ?—help to quieten the pangs of hunger, but they gave an illusion of warmth.

Once again Hinchcliffe—bless his heart !—was the *deus ex machina*. We noticed him followed by his satellites of Company Quartermaster-Sergeants bustling about the camp, stumping off to the lines of the 2nd Scottish Rifles, another regiment of our brigade who were billeted alongside us, and presently saw him return with triumph written on his face. Marvellous man ! By some miracle of barter known only to Quartermasters, he had borrowed us a meal ! Not that it was ready on the instant, still the news was encouraging, and it was not long before orderlies were told off to fetch the borrowed dixies of stew,

How good that stew tasted ! It confirmed the opinion I already held that on a cold, wet day or after a long march the meals the men got from the cookers were better fitted to the occasion than those the officers enjoyed. True, it was ordinarily just " stew "—a nondescript dish, ranking possibly low as a specimen of the culinary art, into which had been put any and all sorts of comestibles that were available and which had often simmered far too long. But it was wet, it was hot, and it was appetising. Whatever the ingredients, it smelt right, and usually tasted good, even if, as sometimes happened, a kipper or two had found their way among the meat, vegetables, biscuits, " Maconochies," and beans. Moreover, it was normally ready as soon as the troops, for even on the Somme actual breakdowns in the Quartermaster's department were rare. By contrast the officers, being privileged beings, had to wait until their mess servants had unpacked their cooking-pots and crockery. Then an attempt was hurriedly made to lay some sort of table. All this reduced the time available for preparing any hot food, so that often, after watching the men gulping down steaming mess-tins of savoury meat, we were constrained after a gruelling march to sit down to a meal of cold slices of bully-beef, to imperfectly heated " Maconochies," or sometimes to rashers of fried ration beef. Certainly we managed to score in the evening when the servants had time to put up a respectable dinner, but whenever we were on the move I envied the men their midday meal.

On this occasion we shared it with avidity, and our outlooks speedily changed as a result. After all, things were not so bad. Here we were, safely in camp, out of the line, and to all intents and purposes out of danger, for the enemy seldom bothered to shell areas so far in rear, while bombing by aircraft was not the terror that flieth by night which it was afterwards to become. Better still, unless rumour was again unreliable, we were going right back for the rest we had hoped for for so long. What had we to worry about ? Let us make ourselves snug and look forward to a " cushy " time ahead. What matter if it was dark by the time we had finished eating ? A few candles and a brazier made the tent look all the warmer.

I wandered down to the Battalion Headquarters tent to have a word with Matheson and see if I could glean any advance information as to our movements. I found him very wroth. The Headquarters mess was worse off than we had been, for though the transport had by now arrived, the Headquarters wagon had not. It was reported to be broken down some miles from camp. Matheson was in no mood to be probed with impunity, and any way the brigade mail had not reached him, so he probably knew no more than the rest of us. I left him and went back to the company tent.

There you behold the three of us once again, sitting on our flea-bags, smoking cigarettes, sipping a very welcome whisky and water out of tin mugs and coughing from the coke fumes given off by the brazier. The wheel had turned full circle. We were back within a hundred yards of the spot whence we had set out a week before. Much water had flowed in the interval. Many lives had been lost, some out of our own immediate circle, but, except that we were demonstrably more cheerful, there was otherwise no difference in our thoughts or conversation. The topic was still the all-absorbing one of what was going to happen next. Were we going out, were we going to stay, or were we going back into the line ? We argued about it and about.

Dinner-time came and went. The rum ration was announced, and I went out to supervise the issue of it myself. This I did personally as often as was possible, not so much from a sense of duty as because I had a sneaking feeling that by so doing I was identifying myself with an important and welcome piece of ritual. It was one way of showing the men that I was taking some interest in their well-being. Besides, I flattered myself I knew the deserving fellows, and saw to it that they got an extra liberal allowance, though I was never a believer in letting any rum go back to store, or in hoarding it for the use of officers. Rum issue was a cheery occasion on even the most cheerless day. Company-Sergeant-Major Scott of course escorted me, and came back to the officers' tent afterwards to join us in a tin-mug of whisky and water.

It was always a joy to have Scott in for an informal talk. Quiet-voiced, phlegmatic to a degree, with sandy hair, ruddy face, and blue eyes, he was the antithesis of the bellowing warrant officer beloved by cartoonists. A man of considerable education and marked gentleness of manner, he got results by the affectionate regard in which he was held by officers and men rather than by obvious resort to discipline. Possibly the fact that he had been for years the best full-back in the regimental soccer teams, and that his gruff humour could be a very cutting weapon were valuable assets ! Except on the football field, I never saw him hurried. Without any especial gifts of command, he managed to be gently but firmly efficient, and one of whom an officer could gratefully say he was at once a trusted subordinate and a faithful friend. Poor Scott ! He got his commission later, but little good it did him. Taken prisoner towards the end of the war, he survived only to be shot in Dublin during the Irish trouble. For the moment he was one of us, and we discussed with him what we would do to pull the Company together as soon as we got back to some training area. After all, we argued, we should have a good chance of preliminary cleaning-up and getting acquainted while we were at the Citadel. We should probably have two or three days with nothing more to do than straighten the tangle into which a unit largely composed of new men under recently-promoted N.C.O.'s was found to get into in circumstances like those in which we had been living for the past week. So we planned, with all the keen enthusiasm of the young officer, arguing the merits of the younger lance-corporals and corporals, the improvements noticed in the behaviour of some of the " tougher " characters, the backslidings of one or two of the more promising.

Miserable mice ! Our fond schemes were destined to go sadly " agley." An ominous rap on the tent—the delivery of Battalion orders—shattered our dreams. Orders were brutally short. One item was enough. " The Battalion will find a working party of 6 officers and 300 men to-morrow, November 16th. . . ."

For a second words failed us. Then with a " Well, I'm . . . ! " we each exploded, bitter anger

striving to get the better of bitter disappointment.
Technically the Division was in Corps Reserve.
Officially on the disposition charts back at General
Headquarters we would be shown as " Resting."
Staff-officers with red and blue arm-bands and
polished field boots were probably saying, as they
scanned the charts, " Good, the 8th Division is
having a rest. They have had a pretty strenuous
time lately." Rest ! The irony of the word.
Here were tired men, men rejoicing on at last being
free of the fears and discomforts of the forward
areas, called upon to parade in the darkness at
6 a.m., to go back into the danger zone and to work
there all day, not indeed as soldiers, but as navvies.
Thus was insult added to injury. The party was
scheduled to work till 4 p.m. and was required to
supply the labour for a decauville railway track
which the sappers were laying at Guillemont, of all
unhealthy places. Nor was just a handful needed.
That would have been tolerable, since the number
might have been found from the fortunate ones who
had stayed at transport lines while the Battalion
was in the trenches. From sheer force of habit,
resignation triumphed over anger. The job had
got to be done.

    " That means seventy-five from us, Sergeant-
Major," I said. " You'd better go and warn the poor
devils before they go to sleep." " The remainder
of the Battalion will parade for baths," I read. What
an anti-climax. " I'll send orders over as soon as I've
written them," I told Scott, and he left us. I turned
to Mac and George. " Apparently one of you two
has to go. I'm sorry. You'd better toss for it."
They did, and Mac won. We both sympathised

with George, who took his bad luck with characteristic Yorkshire stolidness and not a murmur of a " grouse."

Whatever they may have felt, the men received the news in much the same way. The tents being close together, we could not fail to overhear one conversation between a man just warned for parade, and his platoon sergeant. " Do we go by train to that working party to-morrow, Sergeant ? "

" Yes," was the prompt reply, " and don't any of you young soldiers get down to pick flowers on the way, because they've got A.P.M.'s along the line and they'll run you in if you do."

A loud laugh greeted this sally, in which we joined, the idea of flowers growing in such a Slough of Despond being ludicrous in the extreme.

Actually orders had specified that the party should leave by decauville train from the Citadel Station, so-called, which was alongside the Camp. And this was the small measure of consolation we could find as we turned into our flea-bags. It was something to know that at last a light railway was being laid nearer to the line. Our efforts would help to make easier the lot of ration-parties and of the wretched pack animals which now carried ammunition right up to the guns. But the conviction could not be dispelled that somewhere in the Army fresher labour might have been found for the task. And so to sleep.

The departure of the workers did not disturb either Mac or me. Nights in camp were in many ways noisier than in the trenches. There was the continuous growl of distant gunfire, the startling crash as some long-range gun or heavy howitzer

fired from an emplacement close at hand.   There
was the occasional throbbing drone as a night-flying
plane passed overhead, the chug-chugging of motor-
cycles as dispatch riders came and went.   There
were the challenges of sentries, the whinnying and
fretting of picketed animals, the creak and rumble
of moving transport.   Voices called to one another
out of the darkness.   Though half the Army might
sleep, the other half was awake.   Never, as in even
the greatest cities, was there a brief period when all
seemed still.   The war machine knew no rest.

So it was small wonder that the additional noise
of men parading in the lines passed unheard by
us.   Subconsciously we were aware that George
had risen and left the tent, but it was not till three
hours later that we were with difficulty aroused.
And to what a morning did we reluctantly awake !
Winter had stolen upon us in the night, determined
to show that all his previous attempts at " frightfulness " had been child's play.   He had already
demonstrated his powers in the matter of rain.   Now
he would give up a snap of real cold.   At first the
change was not unwelcome.   With our bodies still
warm from sleep and a substantial breakfast, we
could congratulate ourselves that the rain had
stopped.   If it would only keep fine for a day, some
of the mud which washed ankle deep round the tents
might dry up.   Even a hard frost might be prefer-
able to the everlasting torture of wet feet.   But as the
morning wore on and we tried to keep moving about
on self-appointed routine jobs in a half-empty camp,
the cold began to strike home.   God !   How cold
it was !   There was no frost, and but little wind.

But an implacable grey sky seemed to have drawn every element of warmth out of the sodden earth. Soon probably it would snow, and that would be even worse. Had there been any stretch of hard, open ground nearby we could have made an effort to keep warm by organising some " physical jerks " or games of a sort, but the mud lay thick over everything. There was nothing to do but to keep up as much movement as possible until noon brought temporary relief in the shape of a hot meal. Afterwards the depleted company fell in, as detailed in orders, to march to the divisional baths near Meaulte.

It was a joy to get outside the camp boundary and to be moving somewhere with a set purpose, and Mac and I felt our spirits rise with the temperature of our bodies as we set out at the head of the column with our towels and clean underclothes in the pockets of our British warms. Behind us the men sang, a good sign, though the vulgarity of the songs they chose was an even better indication that they were feeling cheerful.

We had now more energy to look about us and to note details of the vast concentration of men, beasts, and machines which spread as far as the eye could see across the countryside. We saw strange-looking guns, great hump-backed howitzers being drawn along by tractors. We looked out eagerly but without success for those new monsters, the " tanks," which had burst so dramatically upon friend and enemy alike at Flers some six weeks before. So far we had not seen one, and our only idea of what they looked like had been gleaned from very foggy newspaper illustrations. We passed through lines of Australians, seeing them at close quarters for the first time, and marvelled at the difference in their physiognomy, their stature, and their equipment. The slouch-hats we knew already, but how odd their shirt-like jackets looked ! We commented on their dirty, slipshod appearance, which we did not then realise masked a deadly efficiency as fighting-men ; and on the curious lope of their long-maned horses. German prisoners were working on the roads under lanky Anzac guards. Few of them were our idea of " Square-heads." Some were mere boys, others myopic be-spectacled scarecrows. Many were bearded, some having fringes of whiskers framing their faces after the manner of the great-crested grebe. All wore the long-skirted field-grey coats, the trousers stuffed into clumsy boots. It gave us a strange feeling to see our enemies at such close range. Except for dead ones, for an occasional miserable prisoner dragged back half-dead with fright from some raid, or for groups seen through field-glasses far behind their lines, many of us had never seen any Germans. That was one of the oddest aspects of the war. There must have been hundreds of men who were in France and in the trenches for months, even years, who never set eyes on the men they were fighting. The enemy early became a legend. The well-wired trenches that faced ours frequently at a distance of only a few yards, gave shelter, we understood, to a race of savages, Huns, blond beasts who gave no quarter, who crucified Canadians and bayoneted babies, raped Belgian women, and had actually built kadaver works where they rendered down the bodies of their dead into fats ! It was perhaps as well that we should believe such tales. But were these pallid, serious youths really capable of such enormities ?

We noticed too, how the tide of mud was flowing rearwards. Even country that had been behind the original battle-line of July 1st had now become engulfed. Not so long ago Meaulte had been a trim village, with its houses thrusting white-washed fronts on the pavé streets. But now the pavé was broken and the streets ran mud, while down them jostled men of every branch of the British Army and of many nationalities. English gunners and supply men, tall " Aussies," stockier New Zealanders, and mournful Germans rubbed shoulders with French infantry and gendarmes, bearded Sikh cavalrymen, and grinning negroes from the British West Indies. Even in such an international medley, drab was the dominant note, and the horizon blue of the French failed to stand out from the more sombre tones of khaki and field grey. Meaulte was one of the bottle-necks through which was fed the flood of men and munitions for the Somme offensive. Here hundreds of regiments and batteries had spent a last night's rest before moving on nearer the line. We had ourselves spent a very uncomfortable twenty-four hours there some three weeks previously. Night after night unit had succeeded unit since the battle began. Morning after morning they had been pitchforked out towards the fires through which they must pass to Moloch. With each departure, the place had become dirtier, lousier, more disreputable. So now the houses, once so neat and well-kept, were foul and rickety, crammed to bursting with troops or commandeered for offices or stores. What was once a cheerful, flagged kitchen, was now a billet, its only furniture the tiers of wooden frames covered with rabbit wire which served as beds for the fifty men who would occupy the room for one night—and then on. A baker's shop had become the office of the French Mission in the area, a grubby tricolour hanging listlessly from the pole outside. Some farm buildings round a midden sheltered the mobile workshops of a brigade of heavy artillery, and 8-inch howitzers stood to have their recoil-buffers repaired where once Percheron plough-horses had waited to be unharnessed.

Toward the end of the village we descried a Foden disinfector, or in the vernacular a " delousing machine," whose function it was to receive the highly-populated undergarments of men coming out of the line, and fumigate these so that, it was hoped, all the live stock, whether actual or in embryo, should perish, and the garments be fit for reissue. In a sense, therefore, the engine stood for modern hygiene, but at the same time the fact that it was necessary at all was a commentary on the changeless-ness of war. Who would have believed that in so short a time youths like ourselves, brought up with all the scrupulous twentieth-century regard for cleanliness and sanitation, could not only be as cheerfully lousy as mediæval mercenaries, but have come to accept the louse as a natural if somewhat irritating companion ? And this, mark you, not-withstanding that many of us had been brought up with the idea that the mere mention, much more the existence, of the domestic flea was a taboo. At the moment the engine was a welcome landmark, in-dicating our destination—a nondescript building before which hung a black notice board whereon, beneath the familiar red square within a white one which was the divisional sign, appeared the words " Divisional Baths."

We filed in, officers to the right, men to the left, groping our way through a steam-laden darkness which a few hurricane lamps and candles were doing their pathetic best to penetrate. If at first our eyes could register but little, our noses were at once assailed by an atmosphere in which the smell of wet clothes and the wash-tub vied with the cloying odour of hot human bodies. As soon as we could see clearly enough to distinguish the particular iron bath or wooden tub in which we were to bathe, we started to undress (a difficult process when there are no chairs or benches on which to sit) grumbling and swearing as we balanced, first on one leg and then on the other, in an attempt to unroll puttees or pull off sodden boots and socks, and at the same time prevent them falling on to the wet floor. Then we grumbled and swore because we could find insufficient places on which to hang our clothes, and again because we could not see where we had put them. Altogether, an observer would not have carried away the impression that we were overjoyed at the prospect of a real wash after so long an abstinence. I doubt if we were. It was certainly not because we were contrasting this gloomy, malodorous cavern with what we remembered bath-rooms to be like, but rather that subconsciously we had gone so long without a bath, without complete and absolute stripping, that our clothes had become part of us, and we shrank from removing them, especially in the middle of a November afternoon some miles away from camp.

Though it was delicious to lie and soak in the steaming, soapy water, and yield to the lassitude that crept over one, it did not somehow seem right. And when our ablutions were over and the men, still sweating, had donned " grey-backs," pants and vests fresh from the " de-louser " and stood ready for the road, how uncomfortable we all felt ! Far from being freshened or invigorated, we were hot and sticky and our new underclothes tickled abominably.

The march back, of course, only made matters worse, and we reached the Citadel thoroughly sweaty and irritated. Cleanliness, I then realised, could be as strange a sensation as dirtiness. Anyway, a three-mile trudge along wet roads on a winter evening directly after a hot bath might be expected speedily to dissipate any pleasurable glow that it had aroused. It is worthy of record that no one caught the chill that might be expected to ensue if the same thing were done under the ordinary conditions of civilisation, especially since by the time we reached camp it was dark and colder than ever, while the man whose boots had kept out the wet was lucky indeed. It is worthy of record, but affords no occasion for surprise, for one of the minor wonders of the war was the astonishing rarity of the common cold in all its objectionable forms. No matter that we remained in sopping clothes in waterlogged trenches in midwinter for days at a time ; no matter that our feet were seldom dry and never warm ; no matter that we slept on the ground or in stuffy underground warrens ; no matter that we were frozen, rained on and snowed on, the rarest thing in France was to see a pocket-handkerchief being used to mop a running nose ! Now why should that have been ? Was it only due to the training, and the open-air life ? Was it only because we could not herd together in overheated, overcrowded theatres, cinemas, or restaurants ? Or was it due in part to the fact that we so seldom had the chance to soak our bodies in hot water ? In other words, might there not be some causal connection between the infrequency of our ablutions and our immunity from colds ?

The bathing parade fell out in the darkness and splashed back to their chilly tents. Mac and I walked back to ours, lit the candles, and sat down to enjoy the tea which, from the strength of it, Purkiss must have been brewing for some time against our return. Had some benevolent fairy then asked us what we would most like to do, we should doubtless have replied, " Get down to it now and get off to sleep while we are still warm." But the thought of being able to do any such thing was so fantastic that it never occurred to us. Which was just as well, as we had scarcely finished tea before the plodge-plodge of men tramping through the lines signalled the return of the working-party. George's hoarse voice could be heard exhorting his men to " Pick 'em up," " Mark time in front," " Halt ! " Sheer force of habit. Poor old George, no exigency of active service could break down the training of years on the barrack square. I sent Mac out to relieve him and see that the party were properly settled in, and teas " dished up." George blundered into the tent, tired, wet, and mud-bespattered, unhooking his equipment as he came.

" Hullo, George ! " I said. " What kind of a day have you had ? Any casualties ? "

" Might have been worse," he replied, surprisingly enough in the circumstances, but then you never knew the depth of his native stoicism.   " No one was hit, but that wasn't the fault of the R.E.'s. Nice kind of a carry-on, three hundred men working like bloody navvies under a couple of R.E. officers and some N.C.O.'s !   If Jerry had happened to shove over any iron rations a good many of us would have been napoo-ed.   But he was very quiet all day. The lads stuck it well too.   Hi, Briggs ! " he yelled. " Tea !   Jildy ! "

" What about a whisky first ? " I suggested.

" Can a duck swim ? " was the prompt reply. " By gum, that's good ! "

And that was all the description I was able to get out of him of a day's work which must have been as depressing as it was strenuous.   His only complaint was the familiar one on the part of the regular soldier, of having to act as unskilled labourer to the Sappers.   From my point of view, the important thing was that he had brought back his party intact and, Mac reported a few minutes later, seemingly in good heart.   Certainly the buzz of conversation and the chuckles of merriment which arose from the lighted tents were not indicative either of excessive fatigue or of low spirits.   But this was one of the remarkable characteristics of the British soldier—when by every law of nature he should have been utterly weary and " fed-up " he invariably managed to be almost truculently cheerful.   Satisfied that there was no more to be done for the present, I felt that perhaps a further attempt to draw the Adjutant as to the future movement of the Battalion was indicated. Slipping on a British warm and winding a woollen muffler round my neck, I sallied forth. The night was already " perishingly cold." These words recur daily in the war diary of the period. It is hard to think of any apter description, or that there have often in recent years been Novembers as cold as that of 1916. There was still no frost, but there was now a relentless north-east wind which cut through clothes or canvas like a razor. The sky was grey and gloomy with a feeble moon struggling to pierce the shifting blanket of clouds. The orderly-room tent was empty save for Greenwood, the Orderly-room Sergeant, who volunteered the information that I should find the Adjutant in the Headquarters mess-tent.

" Do you know if the C.O. is there ? " I inquired tactfully.

" No, sir," was the reassuring answer, " the Colonel has gone to bed."

" Gone to bed ? " I repeated. " Why ? Is anything the matter with him ? "

" I don't think so," Greenwood laughed, " except that he can't get warm. Feels the cold very badly, sir, does Colonel Jack. He was telling the Adjutant that he hardly slept a wink last night, he was that cold."

I then recalled that Cook, the medical officer of the Scottish Rifles, had told me that Jack had spent all his life trying to keep himself down to a riding weight of 10 stone when he should normally have ridden nearer 12 stone, and that these years of weight-reducing had left him without any of the fatty tissue which is Nature's protection against cold. This was the first evidence I had had of the Colonel's difficulty in keeping warm, but the important thing at the moment was that the coast was clear for me to beard Matheson.

I found him crouching round a brazier in the headquarters tent with Raynor, his assistant. The Doctor, heavily wrapped up, was trying to read a book. I accepted Matheson's offer of a drink, hoping by emphasising the social nature of my visit to glean some pearl of information without recourse to the embarrassing necessity of having to ask outright. But there was " nothing doing." For no apparent reason, we were all very cheerful, except the Doctor, to whom the epithet will not apply. We wronged him by imagining he was lugubrious, since we learnt later that he owned an acute, if peculiar sense of humour, but he was never seen to look cheerful. If his nearest approach to a smile was an apologetic twisting of his mouth, his habitually glum expression was the mask to the whole gamut of the emotions. It was not therefore surprising that he showed himself none too pleased at Matheson's repeated admonitions to " cheer up." We laughed and " reminisced " about a variety of topics, but both Matheson and Raynor, whether by accident or design, kept off the subject of our movements. It was getting on towards dinner-time.

" Well, Matty," I said, getting up to go, " I'll have to be pushing off. Thanks for the hospitality. Oh ! By the way, I suppose there is no news about us going out ? "

" Nope ! Not a darned word officially. Every one talks as if the Division was going to be relieved, but I suppose something up in front will happen and put the kibosh on everything."

I was just leaving the tent when Raynor chipped

in with, " What about the brigade lorry to Amiens ?
Weren't you going to say something about that ? "

" Oh, yes," Matheson said ; " I nearly forgot to
ask you. Brigade have got a lorry going in to
Amiens to-morrow for officers who want to do
shopping. They've allotted us three places. Do
you want to go ? "

There was no doubt about my reply. I leapt at
this opportunity, not only because it meant getting
away from the Citadel and its mud for a day, but also
because it was an insurance against being detailed to
accompany any working party that might be ordered
for the morrow. I marched back to my tent with a
much lighter step.

Dinner that night was a cheerless affair owing to
the growing difficulty of keeping warm, and not even
a well-stoked brazier and as many clothes as we
could heap on ourselves sufficed to keep us comfortable. Indeed we sat half in our flea-bags to eat it,
and afterwards got right into them to await the
arrival of orders with our fates for the next day.
Their contents, when they arrived, were neither
more or less than we expected. The main item was
practically a repetition of the night before. " The
Battalion will find a working party, etc." The only
difference was that this time only 200 men and
4 officers would be required, and providentially for
Mac, the officers were this time detailed by name,
none being required from B Company.

After the usual formalities of warning the wretched
men and issuing the rum, we were glad of the excuse
to turn in early and seek warmth under flea-bags
and blankets.

VI

INTO REST

VI

INTO REST

THERE is a wealth of sensuous satisfaction in managing to get snug and cosy amidst bleak and cheerless surroundings. Does not a howling gale in the chimney emphasise the bliss of a warm bed? But that night it seemed that we had no sooner congratulated ourselves on the " fug " we had got up, and resigned ourselves to well-won slumber, than an icy blast and some one shouting in the darkness jerked us back to reality. Alarums and excursions without! The tent flap was open, and Briggs standing in the entrance. What did the commotion mean? If our sleep-drugged minds held any conscious thought it was that the " something " had happened, and that we were for the line again.

" What the devil's up? " I managed to inquire.

" Orders just come in, sir," Briggs said, " that the transport has got to move off at nine o'clock Everything has to be packed by 8 a.m., sir."

We did not appreciate the significance of the words. George muttered thickly, " What the hell next? " Mac only groaned wearily. I asked Briggs to repeat the message.

" Transport has to move off by 9 a.m. All kits, blankets, and heavy baggage to go by it, or the blanket lorry to be packed by 8 o'clock. Orders just come in from brigade, sir."

Slowly the significance of this message dawned on us. Like a thief in the night our reprieve had come. These were surely the orders we had been hoping for for so long. We were, we must be going out ! Yet the realisation made it no easier for us to crawl out of warmth and comfort into the darkness of that bitter November morning.

" What time is it now ? " I queried, too lazy to look at my own watch.

" Five o'clock, sir."

" Oh well, send for Company Sergeant-Major Scott."

While they fetched him I should have at least a momentary respite. I snuggled down again. No matter that I knew full well that I could delay the inevitable by at best a few seconds, the instinct to snatch " just a little longer " in bed was as strong as ever in spite of the joyous news to which we had awakened. Almost at once it seemed, Scott was round and fully dressed. Everything was under way, he reported, but he grumbled a little because the task of packing up was complicated by so many men having to parade for the working party. He was hurrying them on so that they got all their blankets rolled and stacked before they left. The early hour, the darkness, the " perishing " cold, the bustle and confusion of dressing in crowded tents, the struggle of dealing, still half-asleep, with heavy rolls of blankets—these, you might think, would combine effectively to put a damper on any show of light-heartedness. But it was not so. That strange, incalculable British sense of humour shone

like a bright light even in these adverse circumstances. Oaths there were, it is true, and fearful
imprecations as rifles were knocked over on to some
one's stockinged feet ; as some one tripped over a
tent rope and fell headlong in the half-frozen mud ;
or as some one, wobbling under a roll of blankets,
barged into some one else. Yet there were as many
laughs as curses, and no " grouses." And as I
dressed I overheard a snatch of conversation which was
typical of the prevailing spirit. Some one who had
either drawn a " dud" shirt from the " de-lousing"
machine or had missed his bath altogether, had
adopted drastic measures. Said he : " Coom 'ere,
Bill. Just look at this 'ere. Would you believe it,
last night I hung my shirt up outside the tent so as
the frost could kill the ' chats,' but just you take a
pike at 'em now. The little b——r's are still alive,
only they're standing up on their hind-legs, and
clapping their front feet to keep themselves warm."

The goings and comings in the darkness kept
steadily on, until before the working party fell in all
the blankets and heavy baggage, except the one
blanket per man we were mercifully to be allowed to
carry out with us, had been stacked in a noble pile
by the roadside, to await the lorry from the Divisional
Supply Column to come and collect them. Six
o'clock came and the working party moved off—
back towards the line. It was still dark, and very
cold. The camp seemed emptier and more cheerless than ever. Officers' kits were packed and the
servants were carrying them across to transport
lines. What more is there to say ? What was
there to do ? What did we do ? We had now
only the bare boards of the tent or our coats and the

one blanket to rest upon.   It was too cold by far to
settle down again.   So we just stamped up and
down, sat down, got up, smoked, talked, grumbled,
as usual, managed to laugh a little, and speculated on
where we were off to to-morrow.   There was the
fact that we had now a topic of discussion.   Were
we going out for a long rest or merely moving to
another sector or even another battle front ?

Daylight found the question still unsolved.
Breakfasts were served early, as the " cookers " had
to march with the transport at 9 a.m.   Until we
caught up with our transport again, all rations would
have to be issued direct to the men and either cooked
by them in their mess-tins or eaten by them cold and
raw.   The departure of the " cookers " was thus as
shrewd a blow on a winter morning as the removal
of the blankets, for a mess-tin is a poor substitute
for a " cooker " boiler as a cooking utensil.   We
went round the company tents to see that all was
shipshape and that nothing had been left behind,
and then walked across to where Hinchcliffe and
young Greening, the transport officer, looking
absurdly like father and son, were chafing to be
away.   They as much as any one had reason to
rejoice that they were leaving " the Somme " and its
interminable mud-distances, with all the complications of rationing and agony to man and beast that
these involved.   All the time the regiment was in
the line, the transport's day was one of twenty-four
hours, half of which was spent in plodding the weary
way from their camp to Battalion Headquarters
and back again, through traffic, mud, shells, and
rain.   And yet, as I suppose can be said of the
majority of regiments, so efficient were the feeding

arrangements of the army (what a pity that the Operations branch was not as well-directed as the Quartermasters') there was never a time when rations were
not delivered to Battalion Headquarters. If the
troops ever went short, the breakdown in the long
chain came in the last link, that between Battalion
Headquarters and the actual front line. Let us
therefore salute the transport, wish them a good
journey, and a speedy reunion in more congenial
surroundings.

With much straining and pushing, the wagons
bump and squelch out of the juicy mud of the horse-
standings on to the gritty mud of the road. There
goes the headquarter wagon, the bane of Greening's
existence. The designation " G.S." is applied to it
in courtesy only. Actually it is an old railway delivery wagon, pressed, after years of service on
London streets, into Government employ in 1914.
It is a most commodious vehicle, which indeed is the
only reason why it has been retained. It will carry
far more than the ordinary " G.S. " wagon, but
whenever it breaks down, which is often, repairs
take a long time, since spare parts are not available.
Many a time has its fate hung in the balance, but
still it creaks and groans along under its load, drawn
by the two beautiful chestnuts which are the apple of
their driver's eye, and which I am last to see side by
side in death as in life, beside the bridge at Pontavert
in May 1918. The " cookers " clatter out, accompanied by their cooks, whose uniform is almost as
black and greasy as the vehicles themselves. No
smoke curls from their chimneys, for their fires are
drawn. The Maltese cart jogs past, with Brownlow
peering primly from under the hood, followed by the

medical cart. There is more life in the swing and jingle of the limber wagons, their drivers saluting stiffly with their whips as they wheel on to the road past us. Hinchcliffe, looking cherubic as ever on his fat, bob-tailed pony, is a fitting tail-piece. A wave of the hand from him and they are gone. We turn back to our tents. A whole day lies before us, but what to do ?

Luckily the problem did not concern me, as there was only a short time to while away before joining the lorry-party for Amiens. For the first time for a fortnight I was scrupulous about the lustre of my buttons and the shine on boots and Sam Brown belt. Not that these have not been cleaned every day, but simply that, whereas this daily polish was a matter of routine, I was now anxious to look clean and well-turned-out in front of officers from the other regiments of the Brigade. From the geographical point of view, the 23rd Infantry Brigade was a mixed one, comprising, besides the 2nd Devons and ourselves, the 2nd Battalions of the Middlesex and the Scottish Rifles. The clash of dialects was consequently so marked that it sometimes happened that the men of one unit could barely understand those of another. Still, all the Battalions being regular formations brought back from Eastern service, there was a solid core of Cockneys who spoke " pidgin-Hindustani " in each one, so that a sort of *lingua franca* was available in case of difficulties !

I learned from orderly room that I was the only officer from the regiment going with the party, which, on reaching the lorry, I found to include representatives of the Brigade Machine-Gun Company and Trench Mortar Battery as well as of the line

regiments. Only one of them was known to me, a
temporary captain whose regiment shall not be specified. B—— was one of the very few officers I met
in France who conformed to the type popularised by
Journey's End or *All Quiet* . . ., personally gallant,
floridly handsome, and devil-may-care, but a
" soaker," a womaniser, and one whose language was
a string of blasphemies. He was in short one of
those whom Matheson, with true Canadian pithi-
ness, described as " solid ivory from the shoulders
up, with never a thought above his navel." However, for want of any one more congenial, he was an
agreeable enough companion for a short while.
His conversation chiefly concerned the quantity of
liquor he would be able to imbibe during the day, so
I foresaw little difficulty in giving him the slip in
Amiens.

The lorry jerked protestingly in low gear along
the crowded, pitted roads until Albert was reached.
There we craned our necks from under the tarpaulin
hood to catch a glimpse of the Virgin leaning at a
perilous angle from the Cathedral tower. Few of
us had seen this famous phenomenon, though all
were familiar with it from illustrations in the papers
from home.

It was the town's one show-piece. All else was
squalid and depressing. Even in the days of its
prosperity Albert could never have been picturesque.
Now it was in the least attractive stage of decay.
There was something impressive in the remains of a
town or village shattered by shell-fire. For all their
wreckage there was an affinity between them and the
ruins of ancient monasteries in rural England. Indeed, once the tide of war had left them in its wake,

and Nature had covered their scars with a mantle of grass and weeds it was difficult to believe that they had been populous centres a bare two years previously. But the intermediate stage, when the civilian inhabitants had left and the guns had no more than started their work of destruction, was merely depressing. So it was with Albert. Here and there the red-brick artisan's houses had already tumbled into heaps of dust and rubble, but for the most part were still standing. You could truthfully say that " the love and laughter and work and hum of the city were utterly dead," yet though the houses had ceased to be homes they were still tenanted, as the notice-boards showed, by the hundred and one heterogeneous units which clung round the skirts of the army. Their souls had gone with their window-panes, and not even the hessian blinds which flapped over window or doorway could hide their hollowness. Albert was a corpse in which an ichneumon life still lingered.

We steered through the town and out on to the long road which marches straight as a foot-rule between its poplars into Amiens. As the congestion lessened and the surface improved our speed increased. But the worst of lorry riding was that, except for the fortunate ones who had managed to take the seats next to the driver, the passengers could only get a view astern. All we could do was to balance ourselves precariously on petrol tins and watch the road peeling off into the distance behind. Of the surrounding country we could see nothing until it came into our wake. Not that we seemed to be missing much. If the ground was less battered by hostilities than the trench area, the effect was much the same. The hand of war, working with spade and mud, had dealt with it almost as thoroughly as high-explosive. The feeble winter grass had been trampled into the mire under camps and horse-standings. Lorry wheels and cater-pillar tracks had done their work as effectively as the plough. Smoke-blackened incinerators stood where once there had been haystacks. The roadside banks were pock-marked with scooped shelters, dis-figured by tarpaulin lean-to's, on which the bare, grey poplars looked down as if with disfavour. The fields were full of Australian transport and horses, and of the less mobile units of the army services.

We slowed down through Querrieu, where the red and black pennon with its boar's head device proclaimed the residence of the army commander, the man who held in his hands the destinies of the greatest host the English peoples had ever launched to battle. Then on again until the open country gave place to town, and we ran into Amiens, coming to a halt in the square outside the station. We looked about us goggle-eyed. There was not one of us who did not feel a flutter of excitement. Civilisation ! A city with shops, restaurants, and civilian women ! It was for all the world like the thrill of adventure experienced in distant schooldays when school bounds were lifted and we had been allowed in term-time to visit a neighbouring town. We scrambled out, agreed on the hour to rendezvous for the return journey, and split up to go our various ways.

In the succeeding years I was to come to know Amiens well, but this was my first visit, and the im-pression it left on me was one of disappointment.

The first elation born of being again in civilisation was momentary. It evaporated rapidly, leaving me with a feeling that I had been deluded, and that notwithstanding its bustle, its shops, and its civilians, Amiens was really as much an integral part of the battle front as Albert or even Meaulte. The difference was one of degree only, and the air of business and forced gaiety was but a veneer over the real life of the city which was as much preoccupied with war as were we visitors from the mud-belt nearer the Germans. It was only necessary to observe the civilians. The men, as we had expected, were either all in uniform or else stooping ancients and gawky youths too big for their knickerbocker suits. It was the women who were the disillusionment. Young or old, they were almost all garbed in black—how thorough the French are in their mourning, and how they appear to rejoice in it !—and not in black only, but in the roughest kinds of black stuffs, with black woollen shawls, black coarse stockings, black slovenly boots. What a contrast was here with the voluptuous Kirchner drawings we had pinned to our dug-out walls or with memories from our last leave of London shopgirls outside Victoria Station, our first and therefore abiding glimpse of English womanhood, pert, fresh - complexioned, silken - hosed, and neatly dressed ! Who was it had told us that French women were beautiful, or knew how to wear their clothes ? Bah ! these women of Amiens with their flat peasant faces and their shuffling walk were drab bundles of humanity possessing none of those feminine attractions of which we had had our visions. That they were representative of the sturdy soul of

France, mothers, wives, and daughters of her troops, each one of them bowed with past loss or ever-present anxiety for loved ones in danger, we never paused to consider. We had come to Amiens with high hopes. These were not realised. That was all.

There are those who will ascribe our reaction to frustrated carnal desires. (Indeed this aspect of war-time existence has already been emphasised out of all reason.) But it is not the truth. There were not unnaturally many whose animal natures, suppressed during long periods in the line, ran amok at every fleeting opportunity for indulgence. Yet these men would not normally be unduly deterred by appearance. A woman was to them a woman. If good-looking, so much the better, but good looks were only an unexpected pleasure, not an essential. The truth lies far deeper. Our life was not only celibate for long periods, but was one in which all the softer if not the finer influences were absent. It was a rough, dirty life, often lacking the ordinary amenities of peace-time and almost always the more sensuous refinements. It was not surprising, therefore, that Woman stood as a symbol of much that we were missing, and so we came not perhaps to idealise her, but to build up each his own idea of a dream woman, a " woman of the horizon," some one who should be soft, and silken, and scented. As often as not the image might be inspired by nothing more truly beautiful than a drawing of the " chocolate-box " variety in some illustrated periodical. It is not without significance that the song, " The girl I love is on a magazine cover," was popular. The point is that the longing was sensuous as opposed to sensual. And this is indicated by the fact that the shapeless, cart-horse peasant women of Flanders and Picardy, although essentially women, did not satisfy our conceptions. Actually Woman, though a symbol, was not the only one. You could watch the men giving expression to the same feeling in the delight with which they played with the local children. You could recognise it also in the eagerness with which we rushed to buy silk pyjamas, scented soaps, and other minor luxuries whenever we got the opportunity. They were each aids to escape. I, who even at Cambridge had never thought of using bath crystals, found myself buying some in Bethune on coming out of my first tour in the trenches.

Even now one of the excuses for my visit to Amiens was to procure some hair-oil, not the conventional English variety, for that I could have got from the Expeditionary Force Canteen, but the highly perfumed yellow pomade one bought in little glass jars with gold labels. Other requisites were a razor, " cut-throat " type, and some khaki collars. Neither purchase presented much difficulty, except that I learnt to ask for a " 42 " razor and to give my size in collars as " quarante-et-un " instead of 16. As it happened, I should have been better advised to have got my collars from the canteen, for their colour disappeared with the first washing, leaving them an anæmic yellow and bringing down on me an official reprimand for wearing them! Lastly, there was the matter of some drawing materials to supplement the rather grubby sketchbook which I always carried with me, and in particular to attempt to record certain incidents which seemed to merit illustration. I had naturally in mind the observation made to Mac on patrol about " the conscientious objectors firing their recruits' course," and that other retort, overheard at the Citadel, warning workers of the fate which awaited any one who stopped to pick flowers alongside the decauville track.

Though my actual purchases were few, my shopping took me a long time. There was so much to see, so many temptations to squander money. It says something for my self-control that after so long away from shops I did not succumb and buy for the sheer joy of buying. Inquiries of various people during the morning had elicited the information that one might eat well at the Hotel du Rhin, the Belfort, the Godebert, or the Savoy. The last having the added recommendation of a familiar name, we repaired thither to eat an extravagant but not too costly meal, the *plat de resistance* of which was a huge langouste, that clawless cousin of the lobster, about the exact English name of which there was some speculation. It was pleasant to sit down again to a civilised meal in surroundings bordering on the luxurious, but when we came to get up, we found that energy had gone from us. Gone was the eagerness to poke round the shops, the zest in searching for fresh sights. We were content to saunter gently about till the time came for our return. We did, however, inspect " Aux Huitres " and " Charley's Bar " in the quaintly named " Rue Corps Nu sans Teste "—what a smack of the Middle Ages there was about that name !—and the great cathedral rising out of its protective padding of sandbags. But we agreed that Amiens had little to show. Its

restaurants seemed to have impressed us most—
langouste and mayonnaise was a real breath from
another world—and there was no one who was dis-
appointed to leave it when the time came to go.
Even B——, in the words of a Canadian, had "collected such a bun that he was glad to take it home
with him." The impressions left by the return
journey were, like so many lorry rides during the war,
that I was rather uncomfortable and very cold. The
inner warmth and somnolence engendered by a
heavy meal soon wore off, while the biting coldness
of the early morning returned with the dark. The
result was that what with the cold, the jolting of the
lorry, and the petrol fumes, we all felt numb and a
little queasy when we were deposited on the road
outside the Citadel about 6 p.m.

Moreover, it was to a couple of very morose
officers that I returned. Not that this was surprising, for to have been confined to the camp all
day with nothing to do and with no practical means
of keeping warm was hardly conducive to high
spirits. Both Mac and George were huddled in
trench coats and blankets close to the brazier, which
after the manner of braziers was succeeding in giving
more smoke than heat just when warmth was most
needed. Mac nodded towards it. " There's no
coke left, so we've had to burn coal again." The
working party had got back all right, he replied in
answer to my question. " At least our chaps are
all right. They had a rough time. Got badly
strafed several times during the day, and were lucky
only to have two men wounded. Both of A Company, I think."

This was all the news. No orders had arrived, and

nothing more was known as to our movements. There were the usual rumours, possibly more explicit and persistent than usual, that we were going to follow the transport back eventually, but nothing definite as to where we were going or whether into rest or on to some other front. One official document had arrived, and this turned out to be a series of rules and orders issued by the Divisional Commander, a new one whom we had not seen, but who was reputed to be a bit of a slave-driver. These were intended to govern the conduct of battalions in and near the front line. We read them through with growing amusement. " ' Units must arrange that no man remains in the front line for more than 48 hours.' That's a good start, but listen to this. ' Every Battalion moving up to the front must carry up as many trench boards as can be arranged.' ' Every endeavour must be made to construct new and improve existing trenches.' " (" That means picks and shovels," chimed in George. " Yes, and wire and screw pickets," added Mac.) " ' Spare S.A.A. should always be carried for the use of Lewis guns.' ' The danger of trench feet is now considerable. If possible, each man should be supplied with a small bottle of whale-oil for his personal use.' " (" Glory be," exclaimed Mac, " whatever next ? ")

" Anyway," I said, " if we take a trench-board, a bottle of whale-oil, a pick and shovel, a coil of wire, a box of S.A.A. and some mills bombs, and add them to the panoply that Mr. Atkins already has to carry, he will be a sight worth seeing."

" Yes," put in George, " but you've missed the cream of the lot. See here. ' Rifle fire is becoming more important every day.' Damn it all, a bloke

gets few enough chances to use his bundook now !
How in Hell is the poor perisher going to use it at all
if he's got to carry enough for a draught camel ! "

Mac produced a copy of *John Bull* just received
from home. There across the front page was
blazoned the title of the great Horatio Bottomley's
weekly article. " Non-stop to Berlin," it declared.
It was too good an opportunity to be missed. To us
whose experience of the line was so recent, the
spectacle of an infantryman up to his knees in mud,
piled as high with impedimenta as a heavy-weight
furniture remover, yet moving non-stop to Berlin,
was ludicrous in the extreme. Those orders were
a welcome comic relief. The new drawing
materials were dragged out at once, and despite the
cold and the discomfort of sprawling on unyielding
boards, some attempt was made to record the absurdity on paper. Meantime the brazier puffed
smoke, Briggs came and went, apologetically serving
the best meal that Purkiss could manage with his
depleted resources, and the tent grew steadily
colder.

Yet chilled and despondent though we might be,
the servants were in unaccountably high spirits, and
from their tent which adjoined ours, and which did
duty as kitchen as well as sleeping quarters, came
repeated peals of laughter, occasioned by the quick
Cockney wit of Purkiss or the pungency of Parkin's
retorts. Few people got the better of Private
Parkin at repartee. Though the reply might be
slow in coming, it was usually devastating. Was
there not an occasion at a Christmas night jollifica-
tion, when amid the revelry Parkin was sitting silent
and apparently lugubrious. One Drake, slightly

"oiled," went up to him, slapped him on the shoulder, and said :

"Cheer up, Parkin ! Damn it all, what's the matter ? You look as if you were going to give birth to a baby elephant."

A grunt from Parkin.

"Tell me," Drake went on, "what *would* you do if you suddenly did produce a baby elephant ? "

"I'd suckle it," came the reply without a smile or change of countenance.

Parkin was a man of many parts. Asked what his civilian occupation was, he would reply, " I mind a donkey engine at ——'s works, but I don't do much to it. I pay a young lad to do that for me."

"Well, what do you do yourself ? "

"I make a book in my brother-in-law's public," he would answer confidentially. "And it's not a bad game an' all if you know t'ropes."

Certainly he was invariably flush with money, and had a reputation for always winning at cards, which was fully justified. Wherever he went, and he travelled round a good deal during the time he was in France, from A Company mess to Battalion Headquarters, to transport lines, to Brigade or even Divisional Headquarters, he "skinned" every other servant who was venturesome enough to play with him.

As the hours drew on, the noise in the servants' tent gradually died away, and we agreed that we had better turn in. It was the only chance of keeping warm, and, fully dressed, except for our jackets, which did duty as pillows, we rolled ourselves in overcoats and blanket and blew out the candles. But cheated as we had been of a decent meal and

robbed of blanket and flea-bag, our bodies lacked
that store of warmth which might induce sleep in any
circumstances, so that when it did come it was fitful
and restless. Icy draughts through the tent cur-
tains and up through the floor boards kept stabbing
us into semi-consciousness. We turned and turned
in an attempt to ease aching hip-bones or to thaw
our frozen spines. Still we must have been more
soundly asleep than we imagined, for a sudden commotion outside, a thumping on the tent, and the
familiar " Orders, sir," succeeded in bringing us
back to the responsibilities of life no more easily
than normal. I sat up, lit a candle, and took the
folded sheet of foolscap that was shoved through the
flap. " The Battalion will move from the Citadel
to-morrow "—I read on—" Reveille 6 a.m., parade
10.30 a.m., and "—blessed words !—the Battalion
" will entrain at Grove Town station at 12 noon."
Once more glad news had stolen upon us like a thief
in the night. What time *was* it ? Two-thirty a.m.
In other circumstances there would have been a
grouse about the inconsiderateness of the Staff in
sending orders in the middle of the night, but what
did anything matter now ? What were cold boards,
empty stomachs, aching hip-bones, or chilled spines
now we knew we were off ?

" And that's that," sighed Mac contentedly.
" So long as something funny don't happen
before morning," warned George. And with a
feeling of great relief we snuggled down again to
make the best use of the few hours till reveille.
Once banished, sleep was not to be wooed again so
easily, but the knowledge of our reprieve was an

effective counter-irritant to the cold and the discomfort, and the remainder of the night slipped by
rapidly. Nevertheless, the reveille bugle was for
once a welcome sound, and it is no exaggeration that
every one roused himself with something approaching alacrity. There was no dressing to be done, and
though every man who needed a shave made a show
of having one, our ablutions were hardly scrupulous.
Breakfast was a courtesy title, though the tea was hot
and strong and played its part in galvanising us into
full wakefulness.

Since we were moving light, without transport or
heavy baggage, the usual turmoil of packing up or of
striking camp in the darkness was lessened, but there
were other influences at work. The fact that we
were kissing our hands to " the Somme," plus the
uncertainty of our destination, acted on me like
strong drink. It required a conscious effort to
conceal my excitement. No one apparently was
immune, the N.C.O.'s repressing their feelings by
being more regimentally punctilious than usual :
the men, as always when things were going well, by
grousing more than usual. Scott alone gave no sign,
moving unhurriedly about, supervising, checking,
and reproving in his gruff, quiet tones. The job
was complete long before the hour for parade. The
sorry tents in their muddy standings were guyed
tautly and evenly, every scrap of rubbish collected
and taken to the incinerators, the lines cleared as far
" as the mud would allow," in short, the 2nd West
Yorkshire Regiment could take their leave of the
Citadel with the valediction : " Miserable place
that you are, you have sheltered us to the best of
your ability, so, though not loath to quit, we leave

you neater than when we found you, and possibly looking as hospitable as any one could make you."

For the first and last time the Battalion fell in at the bottom of the lines, in full marching order over greatcoats, with blanket in pack and a waterproof sheet over all. Punctually at 10.45 a.m. Colonel Jack gave the command, "Battalion will advance in Companies from the left, D Company leading." And it began to rain. Whether the elements wept at our going or were determined to speed us in the manner to which we had grown accustomed matters not. What was disquieting was that, though it was only a bare three miles to Grove Town, the distance would take us the best part of an hour, and, as we knew too well, men could get very wet in an hour of shambling along crowded roads ankle deep in slush. Worse, Grove Town was a station only in the sense that special R.O.D. trains stopped there. It was not worthy even of the name of siding, and possessed no more shelter than it did platforms ! When, after the usual dreary march, we arrived a little earlier before the hour appointed than would nor- mally be considered sufficient " to catch a train," it would be difficult to imagine a more dismal or deserted spot. The military line appeared to emerge from nowhere out of the wet mist, and to dis- appear towards nowhere into the mist again. We found ourselves on a bleak upland of waterlogged chalk and mud. Below us at a distance of a few hundred yards were the marquees and huts of a big casualty clearing-station, the red-crosses hardly showing up on the rain-darkened canvas. The Battalion halted in the approved manner facing the lines ready to entrain, was told off into sections, and "stood easy." Then as minutes passed and nothing happened, we piled arms and fell out, to stamp about and restore circulations in sodden feet. The hour of noon came and went. Still we stood about near our arms, while the rain coursed in runlets down waterproof capes, spouted off the brims of our steel helmets, and soaked ever more thoroughly into everything we had on.

The fact that the train was late surprised no one. The surprise would have been if it had been punctual. An hour passed and still there came no sign of life from the rails stretching off into the distance. But there is a limit to expectant watching, even on the part of an eager and disciplined body, and gradually the men began breaking up into groups and trying to find something to do. The Colonel recognised the situation and voiced the general opinion when he gave permission for dinners to be eaten—after all, the train might as easily be two hours late as one. The problem of contriving any sort of a meal in such circumstances and surroundings was quite another matter. There was no stone, tree, or corner of masonry as shelter, and though the rain had abated, it still descended in a steady drizzle.

The briefest glance was enough to reconcile us to the necessity of taking our meal standing, as well as to remind us that we should be thankful that we carried food so easily eaten and so filling, albeit so unappetising, as ration biscuits and bully beef. What matter that our chilled stomachs cried for warming drink. What earthly hope was there of warmth?

And the Battalion were actually delving into

haversacks for their bags of biscuits and bully, when
Corporal Robinson achieved his miracle, for which
alone, had he no other claim to fame, his name should
be remembered.   Lying about in the mud were
some logs and splintered pieces of tree trunks.
Under Robinson's direction, his platoon collected a
number of these, and, standing them up, placed
them end to end to form a sort of triangular tunnel,
one opening of which faced the direction from which
the wind was blowing.   Then with infinite care
Robinson whittled with his jack-knife into the heart
of logs where the wood was still dry, and collected the
chips into a little pile to which he added all the old
letters, envelopes, or scraps of newspapers he could
find in his own pockets or gather from his men.

At first no one paid much attention to these pre-
parations.   They were typical " Buggy " antics.
But when his log-pyre was built, and he was on hands
and knees in the mud anxiously applying a match and
puffing at the flame, I wandered over to take a closer
look.   What exactly happened or by what alchemy
he managed it I do not know.   All I can say is that
in a few seconds the puny, carefully-sheltered flame
flickering in the heap of tinder had swelled swiftly
until with a fierce hissing embrace, it had clutched
the soaking logs, and in a very few minutes the
Battalion, open-mouthed, gathered round a bonfire
which both for size and heat would have done credit
to an English village green on a dry Guy Fawkes'
night !   They gathered round, they saw and they
marvelled, as well they might—but it was only B
Company that were invited by No. 7 platoon to use
the blaze for cooking purposes, which, needless to
say, they hastened to do, sections dividing up so that

some men used their mess-tins for bully-stew and others for tea.

The obvious envy of the other Companies puffed me up with pride till I felt very much like the happy monarch in a fairy tale whose court magician has unexpectedly produced a marvel at the auspicious moment. Notwithstanding that I had had nothing whatever to do with it, I identified myself at once with Robinson's triumph, chaffing Palmes and Hawley that they had to come to B Company to be taught how to make themselves comfortable. Palmes indeed, who had had pioneer experience in Canada as well as in Rhodesia, was as much interested in the methods by which Robinson had managed to produce such a blaze as he was quick to congratulate him. Even the Battalion gods in the person of the Colonel and Major Maclaren descended from Olympus so far as to come across and warm themselves. The other Companies quickly set to work to build their own bonfires, but it is worthy of record that it was not until I, with a certain ostentatious magnanimity, had lent Corporal Robinson and presented some incandescent logs that sufficient fires were eventually lit to enable the whole regiment to get a warm, and most of the men to enjoy a meal which was doubly welcome, for not only was it unexpected, but it had had to be worked for. As if in compassionate recognition of our display of self-help the rain stopped. Thus in an incredibly short space of time the whole scene had changed, and from drooping dejectedly about, talking in undertones or not at all, the men regained their spirits and their energy, and laughter and song rose from the circles round the fires. With still no

sign of the missing train, they started wandering
farther afield, especially towards the dripping tents
of the casualty clearing-station, whence one of my
N.C.O.'s hurried back to me with the news that he
had found behind one of the marquees a big dump of
equipment taken from wounded or dead men.   A
lot of this equipment was of the khaki webbing type
which was the active service harness of the regular
army.   When the regiment had landed in France
in November 1914, every man had naturally been
equipped with webbing, but of recent months the
new reinforcement drafts had arrived with the unsightly leather belts and cartridge pouches such as
were issued to Kitchener's Army, until there were
almost as many men with leather as with webbing.
Efforts were constantly being made to discard the
leather, for not only was it clumsy, unsightly, and
difficult to fit, especially when wet, but it was held to
be the badge of the new arrival or the temporary
soldier.   Any tendency on the part of the war-en-
listed man to run down the " old soldier " must be
regarded as a manifestation of an inferiority complex,
for imitation is the sincerest form of flattery, and the
desire of every one to possess a suit of web equipment must be put down largely to the desire to
resemble as nearly as possible the " real soldier."

Here then was a chance, my N.C.O. whispered, to
fit out probably the whole of B Company with the
coveted webbing.   Might he have my permission ?
It was no sooner asked than given, but the news
seemed to pass quickly round the Battalion, so that,
although we had a good start, there was in a few
minutes something in the nature of a stampede towards the casualty clearing-station.   There you have

the interesting spectacle under the conditions that prevailed of men jostling and struggling good-naturedly to seize sets of saturated equipment with as much zest and energy as if they had been competing for dips in the bran-tub at a parish bazaar. The discovery of that dump was a godsend, for not only did it enable us to reduce the percentage of leather equipment, but it kept the troops enthusiastically employed.

While the men hunted for kit, or cast around for other forms of salvage, the officers drifted into groups and talked. The satisfaction of food and warmth had so successfully banished all discontent at the non-arrival of the train that it ceased to be a topic of conversation. The casual observer might have been pardoned for thinking we were content to remain at Grove Town indefinitely.

Palmes, in a very efficient-looking trench coat, laughingly threatened " to knock my block off "—a favourite expression of his—for a libellous sketch I was able to make of him, and from this unpromising opening, the conversation somehow drifted by way of casualty clearing-stations in general, and the one beside us in particular, to the employment of conscientious objectors. Some one suggested that they should not be put in gaol but pressed into the R.A.M.C. for service in casualty clearing-stations and base hospitals, thereby releasing R.A.M.C. personnel with less troublesome consciences for more vital work. Palmes agreed, and proceeded to enlarge on the subject, and we, because he was ten years older than the average of us subalterns, because he had " done things," including breaking virgin soil to the plough in two continents, because he had read deeply, and because in the silence of the open spaces he had thought seriously, were content to listen to him. He spoke with one having authority, and he said, sucking at his pipe :

" I don't understand what is meant by the term ' conchy.' If it means a chap whose conscience objects to war, well, damn it, I am a ' conchy.' You don't suppose I like this show. Its such an infernal waste of time. Besides, I'd rather be farming.

" And if by ' conchy ' you mean a so-called pacifist, I still don't understand. A pacifist may be merely some one who is in favour of peace. But so am I. Very much so. But really you don't mean either of these things. Your ' conchy ' or ' pacifist ' is a man who says in effect ' I want peace. I won't have war. And if we have war, I will have nothing to do with it.' And that of course is absolute tosh. Pacifism put that way means nothing. After all, there is no peace in life. Whether you live in Blackpool or Bulawayo, Amiens or Athabasca, or anywhere else ; whether you live a decent life farming, or grub for money in an office, you've got to fight for your corner, and fight all the time—that is if you mean to keep your foothold, let alone progress. The only time you are at peace is when "— pointing with his pipe stem at the cemetery that was growing up outside the casualty clearing-station— " they shove you underground, and then they very properly put R.I.P. over you !

" Did you ever hear anything so bloody silly as the chap who says, ' I won't fight.' Let him refuse. All I know is that a nation composed of chaps like that will not stop war. It will just be easy meat for one like the Boche or any of the Oriental races who have no illusions about the need to fight for their place in the sun. It's no use your refusing to fight if some one more virile picks on you ! He'll take what he wants from you by force just the same, and your pacific conscience won't save you from getting a kick in the pants or an aeroplane bomb dropped on your block !

" It's better to face up to it, and be ready to defend your life and your heritage rather than lie down and bleat about peace while some one walks roughshod over you."

At the time we only felt that Palmes was expressing very succinctly sentiments with which we all agreed, even if we had not thought of them in quite the same dispassionate way, but I have tried to record his remarks as fully as possible since they seem to have a special significance in these after-days. Gathering resonance with the years, they echo out of the mist and mud of that Somme upland with all the force of prophetic warning. What would Peter Palmes, farmer by nature, and warrior by necessity, have had to say could he have lived into the post-war era and seen how Youth attempts to ensure peace by refusing to look on reality. Are we not as a nation behaving very much like the small boy who, alarmed at noises in the dark, will cover his head with his bedclothes lest he see that of which he is terrified ?

" Damn all ' conchies ' anyway," Palmes went on cheerfully. " We're running this war all wrong ! You've never heard of my famous plan have you, Nansen," he inquired of Maclaren, who had strolled up to join the group. " I'd get thousands upon thousands of miles of barbed wire and build a huge belt, miles wide, from the Swiss frontier to Dunkirk. In other words I'd wire brother Boche in completely. I'd leave outpost sections with guns and machine-guns at all commanding points, to sweep the wire and keep it from being cut too easily, and also plenty of labour battalions to keep on adding to the wire. But all the rest of the ruddy army I'd march away and put to——"

The great scheme was never unfolded in detail. A distant whistle cut him short. Simultaneously the Regimental Sergeant-Major and the four Company Sergeant-Majors all started bawling " Fall in ! Fall in there ! " Officers and men trotted back to form up round their piled arms as the train, drawn by an R.O.D. locomotive which bore a suspicious resemblance to one of those of the Great Central Railway, panted laboriously to a standstill before us.

It was just on 4 p.m. We had waited four whole hours, and not all of them had been unhappy or even depressing.

The train was neither better nor worse than the usual sample of French troop train. For the men, trucks—" Chevaux (en long) 8 : Hommes 40 "— some of them with straw ; for the officers, a coach of first-class carriages. Lest the latter may seem unduly luxurious by comparison with the men's trucks, let me hastily add that the coach had been a very old one before it had been commandeered for military purposes. Since then it had suffered sadly, not least in the matter of windows, and there was not a carriage but had one or two panes broken. The upholstery too was torn and soiled. Yet, though tattered and grimy, the lace antimacassars were still in place. Why was it that that typical piece of French decoration always seemed to remain intact no matter to what ill-treatment the rest of the carriage had been subjected? Actually therefore there was little difference in degree of comfort between officers and men. We had cushions, mostly without springs, and nothing to keep out the night air. The men rode harder, but could at least generate some warmth from their own bodies behind closed doors.

We climbed in with the nearest approach to alacrity we could muster, and such was our preoccupation with making our temporary quarters as comfortable as we could that no one of us had the imagination to lean out of the window and take a last look at the " Somme," to listen to the muffled drumming of the guns, or watch their flashes stabbing the oncoming dusk. We were still arranging ourselves to the best advantage, when, without warning, there was a grating of wheels on rusting lines, and we were off.

It was only then that we became sensible of our damp and mud-plastered condition, which obtruded itself not only in the shape of feet which became rapidly like blocks of ice, but in the stale, sickly odour of wet clothes and the mud itself. We had lived with it and in it for so long that we had ceased to notice it till the mere fact of being in a railway carriage again brought it back to our nostrils. The explanation was probably that, noses being the keenest aids to memory, we sought unconsciously but in vain for the familiar smells of English railway travel, only to register infallibly the " bouquet des tranchées " we had brought with us.

Not that any reference was made to this phenomenon. The business in hand was to get comfortable. For this the first requisite was a light
and, George producing a stub of candle, this was lit
and stuck on the top of a steel helmet. No matter
with what care we shielded it from draughts it re-
peatedly went out, and even while it remained alight
it flickered and guttered abominably. Nevertheless its uncertain gleams were sufficient to allow us
to hunt through packs and haversacks for any forgotten or closely hoarded scrap of provender, and
the search yielding nothing more exciting than a
bar or two of chocolate and the inevitable biscuits
and bully, these were duly eaten and washed down
with the last drops of whisky in our water-bottles.
Though this took time it must not be thought that
the train was bowling merrily on its way. Far from
it. War-time journeying on the French railways
was always an affair of starts and stoppages, but at no
time or place during the whole war was it worse than
in the Somme area during that winter of 1916.
Every few minutes the train would grind and
shudder to a standstill. It might remain stationary,
its engine gently exhaling steam or whistling in a
tone of plaintive inquiry, for any period from a few
seconds up to half an hour, then with a jerk and a
groan, creak onwards for a few more hundred yards.
We soon wearied of poking our heads out of the
windows each time to see where we were, for there
was nothing to see. We never seemed to halt at a
station, and the only exhibit would probably be an
aged and hirsute French railwayman, armed with a
little trumpet on which he would toot, or who would
attempt to harangue our engine-driver from the rear-

end of the train. Besides, now that the first excitement was ebbing, the craving for sleep was stealing
over us, sapping minds and bodies of their energy.
We were short of sleep and were not to be denied,
so each one of us independently loosened his
puttees, unbuttoned his jacket, curled up in his
corner in such a way that his trench coat would cover
feet as well as shoulders, and with pack or helmet as
pillow soon passed into a fitful slumber.

It is meet here to interpolate a word in praise of
the steel helmet. Æsthetically it was a failure—
though not so mediævally hideous as the coal-
scuttles worn by the enemy—but though it might be
less graceful a headgear than the French equivalent,
it more efficiently fulfilled the protective purpose for
which it was designed. The beauty of it was that it
could also, as you have seen, be used when occasion
demanded as a candle-stick, or, without its lining, as
a washing-bowl. Inverted, it was equally service-
able as a pillow or a seat. Indeed, most of us at some
time during the wait at Grove Town had eased our
legs by sitting down on our helmets.

Hour succeeded hour as the train jerked and
clattered through the night, and we snored, turned,
half awoke, rearranged ourselves, and dozed off
again. Nobody would pretend that we were comfortable, but we must have slept for quite respectable
stretches because we had no idea of the passage of
time. Yet we were vaguely conscious always of the
spasmodic lurching of the train and the noises outside whenever it stopped. At the big junction of
Longeau, outside Amiens—little did we dream that
we should know this same station in daylight two
years later when it would be under shell-fire from the

enemy we had now pushed back at such a cost !—
we were properly aroused to consciousness by a
demonstration of the musical shunting so dear to our
gallant allies. So far as we could judge from the
sounds and the flashing of lamps in the darkness,
the procedure was for the shunter to blow a ta ! ta !
ta ! on his trumpet for the operation to begin.
When the backing train was a few yards from the
trucks to be coupled, he would yell " Arretez ! " and
blow a quick blast. These vocal and instrumental
efforts were entirely lost on the engine-driver, who
almost inevitably waited till, with a resounding
crash, he had run into the stationary vehicles
before he applied his brakes. It was an interesting
sidelight on the Gallic mind, but then, as Mac
observed with a yawn, " What can you expect
of a country where even the butcher and the baker
blow some musical instrument when they come
to your door ? "

Even had we then known that Longeau was an
important railway junction just outside Amiens, we
should have been none the wiser as to our destination or the direction in which we were proceeding, so
little did the ordinary company officer, let alone the
rank and file, know of the movements of his own
unit or the lie of the land " behind the front."
(Later, during a temporary attachment on the staffs
of the brigade and division, I was to realise the truth
of this still more forcibly.) At the time, the shunting about at Longeau was merely a peculiarly prolonged and irritating disturbance in the long series
of disturbances that kept jerking us back to wakefulness, or so it seemed, each time we managed to
doze off.

At last there came a halt accompanied by English voices shouting in the darkness, followed by the sound of carriage doors banging. Wearily we roused ourselves. Lights showed here and there, but it was still night. The familiar ringing tones of the Regimental Sergeant-Major, " Come on, there ! All out ! All out ! " removed any uncertainty. We had reached our destination, wherever it might be.

Sleep-drugged, leaden-footed, with our vitalities at their lowest ebb, we made clumsily hasty efforts to collect our scattered paraphernalia, forced unwilling fingers to buckle on equipment, and almost fell as we dropped from our compartment on to the permanent way. Followed a jostling and pushing in the gloom, men elbowing their way towards the voices of Company Sergeant-Majors raised in a medley of " D Company, this way ! " " Fall in here, A Company ! " " B Company, fall in here, B Company ! "

Where the hell *were* we ? As we blundered towards the sound of Scott's voice we passed a station notice-board whereon by the wobbling light of a hanging lantern we read the one word " OISEMONT." Where was Oisemont ? What was it ? The unasked question was answered by the thought, Why worry ? We were obviously far from the battle-zone, witness the fresh keen air which blew sharply on our faces and sent shivers down bodies a-chill after the night's inaction. Still in a torpor, we took our places with the Company, registered rather than heard the command to move off, mechanically repeated it, and found ourselves on the march. Our footsteps, faltering at first, quickly gained in vigour, till they rang bravely on cobbled setts, echoed through the village and crunched out on to a crisp, firm road where the before-dawn wind blew stronger. Let it blow ! By now we were awake, action had restored our circulations, and the wind had no longer any power to numb us. Instead it came as a breath of deliverance out of the night, reassuring us of the existence of green fields, and copses, and farmsteads with smoking cowsheds and all the thousand-and-one sights of the countryside which we could not yet see with our own eyes.

Slowly but surely our spirits rose. The march had begun in silence, then a few muttered remarks, soon a rising flow of conversation, conjecture, and chuckles. And as we marched, the sky began its imperceptible change from dull black to that queer translucent grey. Dimly we were aware that our path lay between the shoulders of hills that humped up above us, dark shapes that made me think of the English Downs in prehistoric ages. The light grew steadily stronger. We saw everything in varying tones of grey, save where the road ran white through the chalk. Soon colour would appear.

Meanwhile a spasm ran through the column, like the contraction of a concertina or the ripple of buffer hitting buffer as a goods train shunts backwards. There had been a momentary halt in front, and as we moved on we passed a figure attended by stretcher-bearers lying on the grass—Yes ! by God, we could see it was green !—by the roadside. " Sergeant Greenwood, the Orderly-room Sergeant, sir, has fainted," explained Scott.

It was now nearly light. We could see clearly

about us, found that we were in country indeed, still
the same downland country of the Somme, but with
what a difference. We needed no eyes to tell us
that it was unscarred by battle, but more welcome
still, we could detect no trace of it having been fouled
and spoilt by military occupation. The fields bore
no marks of encampments, no incinerators with their
piles of charred tins ; the cottages no notice-boards
or billeting signs. Instead, comfortable farmsteads
with buff walls of crude lath and plaster, with strings
of dried beans rustling under the eaves, nestled amid
trees in the folds of the hills. Each, after the
manner of French farms, was built around three
sides of a square, the centre of which was the manure
heap and general refuse dump, from which the
house and outbuildings were separated by a cobbled
causeway. As we passed one, more dilapidated than
the rest, which stood on the roadside, Scott, marching
at my side, jerked his thumb towards the walls
underneath whose cracked plaster the lath frame-
work could be seen in patches, and quietly said :

" It seems to me, sir, that the way they build a
farm in France is to put up a lot of sticks and then
throw muck at them. What sticks is the house.
What falls down is the midden."

We marched on, keenly alert to each fresh,
welcome sight, scent, and sound. Just as the sun
tried to force its way through the morning sky, the
road dropped between high hawthorn hedges, behind which sheltered apple orchards and tilled
fields. A score of magpies, flirting their beautiful
tails, rose scolding us, and winged away on their
dipping flight. And on the outskirts of the tiny

hamlet which was to be our home for a month of glorious recreation, an ass, a patient domesticated farmyard ass, and none of your military mules, poked his rugged head over a gate and brayed us a long and hearty welcome.

Other Greenhill books include:

T. E. LAWRENCE IN WAR AND PEACE
An Anthology of the Military Writings of Lawrence of Arabia
Edited and Presented by Malcolm Brown
ISBN-10 1-85367-653-5
ISBN-13 978-1-85367-653-6

THE GREAT WAR
Field Marshal von Hindenburg
Edited and Introduced by Charles Messenger
ISBN-10 1-85367-704-3
ISBN-13 978-1-85367-704-5

INFANTRY ATTACKS
Irwin Rommel
Introduction by Manfred Rommel
ISBN-10 1-85367-707-8
ISBN-13 978-1-85367-707-6

SAGITTARIUS RISING
Cecil Lewis
ISBN-10 1-85367-718-3
ISBN-13 978-1-85367-718-2

TANK RIDER
Into the Reich with the Red Army
Evgeni Bessonov
ISBN-10 1-85367-671-3
ISBN-13 978-1-85367-671-0

RED STAR AGAINST THE SWASTIKA
The Story of a Soviet Pilot over the Eastern Front
Vasily B. Emelianenko
ISBN-10 1-85367-649-7
ISBN-13 978-1-85367-649-9

Greenhill offers selected discounts and special offers on books ordered
directly from us. For more information on our books please visit
www.greenhillbooks.com. You can also write to us at Park House,
1 Russell Gardens, London, NW11 9NN, England.